Corrective Reading

Enrichment SRA Blackline Masters

Decoding A   Word-Attack Basics

Siegfried Engelmann
Gary Johnson

McGraw Hill SRA

Columbus, OH

SRAonline.com

 SRA

Send all inquiries to this address:
SRA/McGraw-Hill
4400 Easton Commons
Columbus, OH 43219

ISBN: 978-0-07-611213-5
MHID: 0-07-611213-6

4 5 6 7 8 9 MAL 13 12 11 10 09 08

The McGraw·Hill Companies

Contents

Contents

Corrective Reading
Decoding A
Enrichment Blackline Masters

Note to the Teacher

The activities in this book reinforce the skills taught in the 2008 edition of the *Corrective Reading Decoding A* program. Each activity provides practice in an essential reading skill, such as

- recognizing the sounds of letters in isolation and in words
- matching and writing letters (referred to as "sounds")
- discriminating one sound or word from others in a list
- completing words with missing letters
- reading and copying words
- reading words in lists
- reading sentences
- copying sentences

(Skills are identified at the bottom of each page.)

The materials are designed to be completed as study-time homework assignments. The Blackline Master pages correspond by lesson number to the Decoding A lesson numbers. The Blackline Masters should be assigned as homework on the <u>same day</u> that the corresponding lesson is <u>completed</u> at school. The first Blackline Master homework assignment appears at Lesson 11.

Students should be able to complete the homework assignments without any special instructions from the teacher or from a parent. Most exercises parallel those that appear in the regular program. Directions for each exercise appear above the exercise. After you pass out the Blackline Master homework assignment, read the directions for each exercise aloud to students before they take the assignment home.

New exercises appear for the first time in these lessons:

11 Match sounds
11 Circle a sound in a row of other sounds (discrimination)
11 Match and complete words with missing letters
11 Match and copy words
11 Match words with pictures
20 Home reading of word lists
24 Home reading of sentences
34 Circle a word in a row of other words (discrimination)
38 Circle one of three sentences that describes a picture
48 Matching completion: Draw the match line before completing the word
50 Copy sentences

Read-at-Home Activities

To provide additional practice in building oral reading fluency, someone at home listens to the student read aloud. This activity begins at Lesson 20. The student reads aloud rows of words. If the student makes no errors in a row, the parent/listener makes a check mark in the box at the end of the row and signs at the bottom of the page. The student brings the signed page to school on the next school day as part of the daily two-page homework assignment.

Starting at Lesson 24, the student reads rows of words and sentences at home. The parent/listener makes a check mark in the box if the student reads all the words in the row or sentence correctly.

Checking Homework

The homework should be checked each day. The most efficient procedure is to conduct a teacher-directed group work check.

- For each activity, identify the part, and then read the answers from the annotated answer key beginning on page 111 of this book.
- For exercises that provide practice with single sounds or sound combinations, such as matching and copying sounds and circle-the-sound exercises, refer to each letter or letter combination by its corresponding sound.
- For exercises that require students to fill in the missing letters in words, refer to the letters by their corresponding sounds. (For example: *Cats.* What missing sounds did you write? *t, sss.*)

Homework Chart and Point System

Keep a record of the completed homework assignments. A reproducible Homework Chart appears on page viii. You may have students record points on the Point Chart that appears at the top of each *Decoding A* Workbook lesson. Points earned for the homework assignment can be recorded above Box C in the regular Workbook Point Chart.

Points could be awarded as follows:

completing homework	2 points
0 errors	2 points
1 or 2 errors	1 point
more than 2 errors	0 points

When the read-at-home activities begin at Lesson 20:

completing the homework	
reading checkout	2 points

If you award points for homework assignments, you will need to modify the total number of points students can earn in the regular program. (For a discussion of points, see "Awarding and Recording Points" in the *Decoding A Teacher's Guide*.)

An alternative procedure would be to make the points earned for homework assignments separate from those earned in the regular program and to provide special incentives for completing homework.

The Blackline Master homework pages are designed so that students can be successful. Once students learn that they can complete homework successfully, they will be motivated to continue to do so. If the teacher provides positive verbal feedback about completing homework assignments, along with the use of points, students will be encouraged to do well, and their reading performance will continue to improve.

Letter to Parents

A letter explaining the general procedures for homework assignments appears on the following page. This letter should be sent home along with the first homework assignment.

Dear Parents,

Students are expected to complete homework as part of their reading lessons. The homework activities provide practice in essential reading skills. In the daily homework exercises, students receive practice in the following reading skills:

- recognizing the sounds of letters in isolation and in words
- matching and writing letters (referred to as "sounds")
- discriminating one sound or word from others in a list
- completing words with missing letters
- reading and copying words
- reading words in lists
- reading sentences
- copying sentences

The homework activities begin after the students have completed Lesson 11 in their regular book at school. The first homework assignment is Lesson 11. Each homework assignment consists of two pages. Starting at Lesson 20, the student will read a list of words to you. The list appears at the bottom of the second page. For each row of words, make a check mark in the box if the student makes no errors in the row.

Starting at Lesson 24, the student will read lists of words and sentences to you. Make a check mark in the box if the student reads all the words in the row or sentence correctly.

Here are the kinds of errors a student could make:

- saying the wrong word or mispronouncing a word
- adding a word
- leaving out a word
- adding an ending to a word (for example, reading "cats" for *cat*)
- leaving off an ending (for example, reading "fin" for *fins*)
- rereading part of a sentence

After the student reads to you, sign at the bottom of the page. The student should bring the two-page homework assignment to school on the next school day.

Remember to be patient. Students who try hard need to know that they are improving. Your assistance each day will help the student improve. The more practice the student receives, the faster the student will become a better reader.

Thank you.

Corrective Reading   Decoding A Homework Chart

Teacher _____   Group _____

Student	Date																																										
	Lesson Number																																										

Part 1
Draw lines to match the sounds.

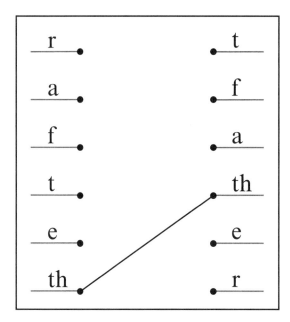

r   t

a   f

f   a

t   th

e   e

th   r

Part 2
Write in the missing letters.

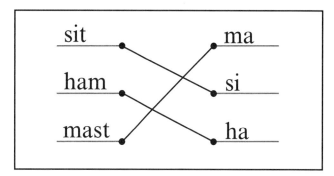

sit   ma

ham   si

mast   ha

Part 3
Draw lines to match the words and pictures.

feet

cat

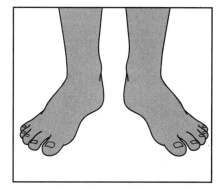

Sound/symbol relationships, word completion, word recognition

Name _____

Part 4

Circle the sounds.

(th) r h d th i m d h e r h th a s m d e   (4)
    m th s m h t e r d a th m h t i r s

(c) i a m d c t e s d a i t c a f r i t m   (4)
    d a t i e f i d c a i m t s i a c d t

(f) i f r d a f o d i e d r f t h m r s f   (7)
    r d c i f a c d i r s f d i c f t h a

Part 5

Follow the lines and copy each word.

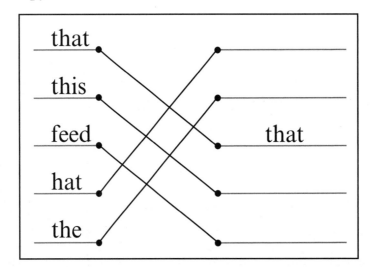

that

this

feed   that

hat

the

Sound/symbol relationships, copying words

Part 1

Draw lines to match the sounds.

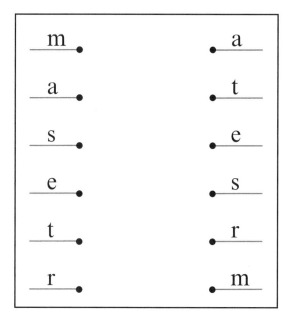

m   a

a   t

s   e

e   s

t   r

r   m

Part 2

Write in the missing letters.

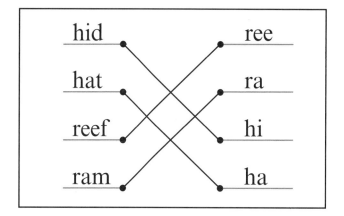

hid   ree

hat   ra

reef   hi

ram   ha

Part 3

Draw lines to match the words and pictures.

ram

hat

rat

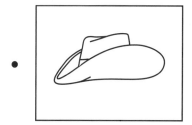

Sound/symbol relationships, word completion, word recognition

Part 4

Circle the sounds.

(sh) sh a t h e m i h a sh t h i s e m h ⑤
e sh a m h sh s i e sh a h t r a s t

(th) s th a t i s h a e th a s e h t f i a ③
h a t e th e h s e m t s e r s h a e

(h) t a t i h c d i a d r h a i t h e c o ⑤
r t o i h o i t c r o f d i a h m r d

Part 5

Follow the lines and copy each word.

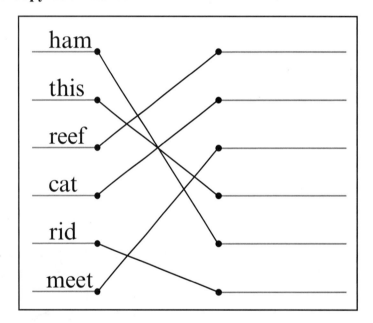

ham

this

reef

cat

rid

meet

Sound/symbol relationships, copying words

Name _____

Part 1

Draw lines to match the sounds.

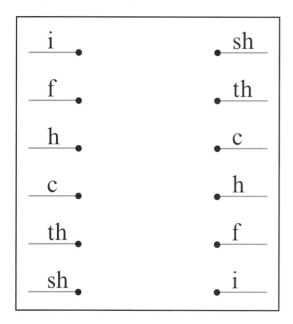

i   •   •   sh

f   •   •   th

h   •   •   c

c   •   •   h

th   •   •   f

sh   •   •   i

Part 2

Write in the missing letters.

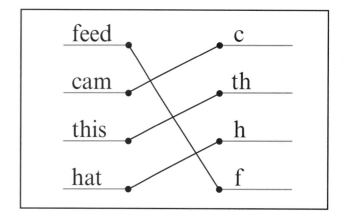

feed   •   •   c

cam   •   •   th

this   •   •   h

hat   •   •   f

Part 3

Draw lines to match the words and pictures.

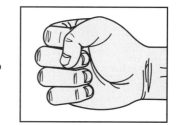

mitt   •

fist   •

mast   •

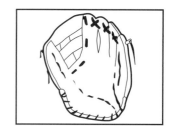

Sound/symbol relationships, word completion, word recognition

Name _____

Part 4
Circle the sounds.

(f) t h i t f i m i d i f c t r i a e i f
     e f m i m i f i f c e f d i h t a m   ⑦

(th) t s h i p a th a e th a s e h t f p i
      h i th a h e h s a e m th e a r s t m   ④

(sh) h e t sh e d i e d sh e i t h i t c r
      r t o c r i sh e r sh s i e h c sh d i   ⑤

Part 5
Follow the lines and copy each word.

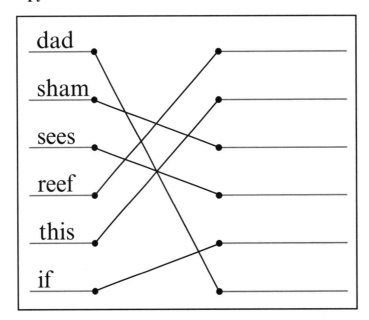

Sound/symbol relationships, copying words

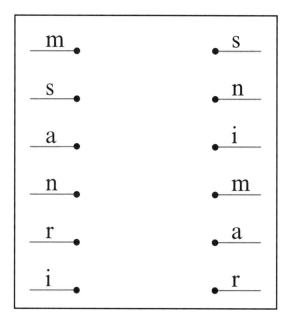

Lesson 14

Name _____

Part 1
Draw lines to match the sounds.

m   s

s   n

a   i

n   m

r   a

i   r

Part 2
Write in the missing letters.

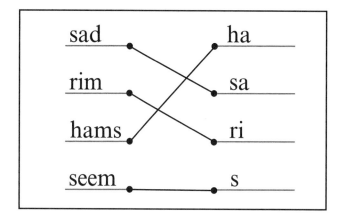

sad   ha

rim   sa

hams   ri

seem   s

Part 3
Draw lines to match the words and pictures.

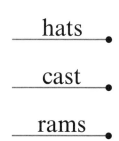

hats

cast

rams

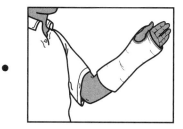

Sound/symbol relationships, word completion, word recognition

Name _____

Part 4

Circle the sounds.

(d) d s i a s i m i s i d s a s i d a m s e   (8)
     e d s i m s d i d i e d s i s a i e d m

(c) e s f i p a c f a e c f a s e f c i e s   (6)
     f i c f a f e f s a e m c f e a p f a c

(n) a m i n a d i a d s n a i n m n d a o r   (7)
     r m o s n o m a r o i n s i a n m s i d

Part 5

Follow the lines and copy each word.

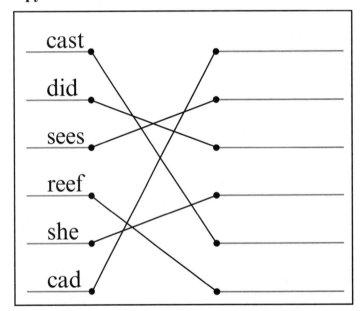

cast
did
sees
reef
she
cad

Sound/symbol relationships, copying words

Name _____

Part 1

Draw lines to match the sounds.

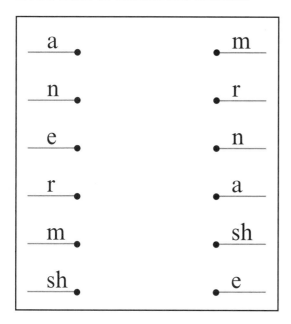

a   m

n   r

e   n

r   a

m   sh

sh   e

Part 2

Write in the missing letters.

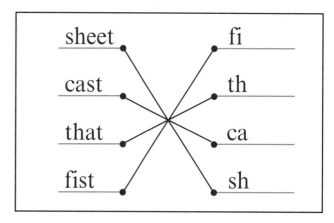

sheet   fi

cast   th

that   ca

fist   sh

Part 3

Draw lines to match the words and pictures.

man

cats

fish

Sound/symbol relationships, word completion, word recognition

       Lesson 15   **9**

Part 4

Circle the sounds.

(r)   m r e a r e m f r i m s a r e m a s

     e m r e m r m a m e i m i e r a i m   (7)

(sh) c sh i p a t h a e sh a e sh c h p

     h i sh a h e h s a e m t h e a i sh   (5)

(a)   a h i n a m e a m s n a i r h m e n r

     r h e s n t h a r i n s i a n m h t s i   (6)

Part 5

Follow the lines and copy each word.

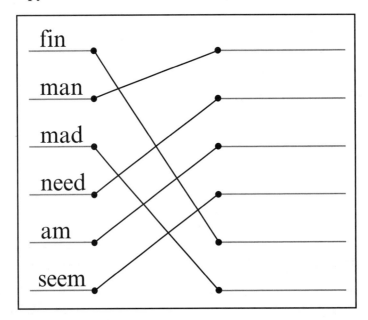

Sound/symbol relationships, copying words

Name _____

Part 1
Draw lines to match the sounds.

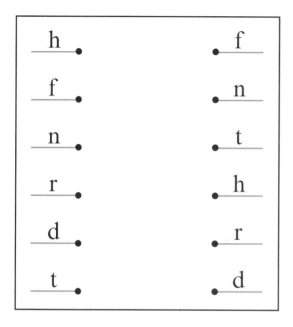

h	f
f	n
n	t
r	h
d	r
t	d

Part 2
Write in the missing letters.

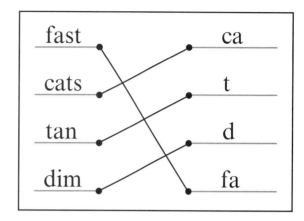

fast	ca
cats	t
tan	d
dim	fa

Part 3
Draw lines to match the words and pictures.

cat

can

feet

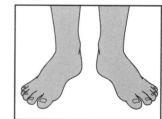

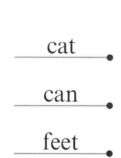

Sound/symbol relationships, word completion, word recognition

Name _____

Part 4

Circle the sounds.

(e) h d e a r e h e d a h m a d e f d r
    e h d e f d t i h e i h r e d a i h t   (8)

(t) c t h i p a c h a i t h a i t h c h p
    h i t h a h i h t a i m t h i a s h m   (6)

(n) a h e n a n e a m s n a e n h m s a
    r h i s n t h a r f e n s e a n r h t   (7)

Part 5

Follow the lines and copy each word.

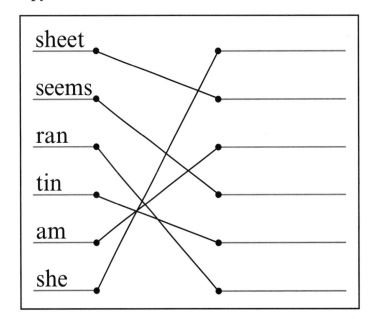

Sound/symbol relationships, copying words

Name _____

Part 1

Follow the lines and copy each sound.

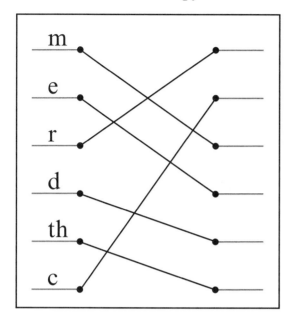

m
e
r
d
th
c

Part 2

Write in the missing letters.

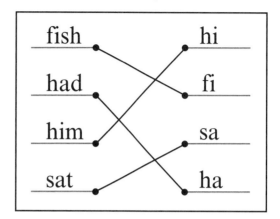

fish   hi
had   fi
him   sa
sat   ha

Part 3

Draw lines to match the words and pictures.

she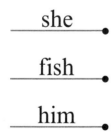

fish

him

Sound/symbol relationships, word completion, word recognition

Name _____

Part 4

Circle the sounds.

(n) n d e a m e n e t h e n d a t e n d m (7)
     e n t f n d t e m e i n d r d a e a f i

(f) t f e p a c f a e t c f a r t f c p e (7)
     r e t f a i e f t d e m t f e n d i t r

(h) a t i h a h i a h s f a i h t a c d t (7)
     r t c s h d t a r t i h s i a h i s r a

Part 5

Follow the lines and copy each word.

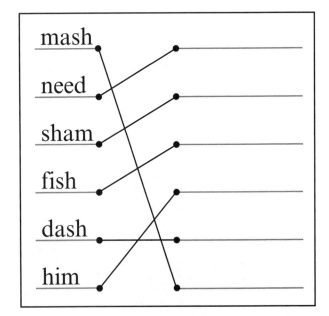

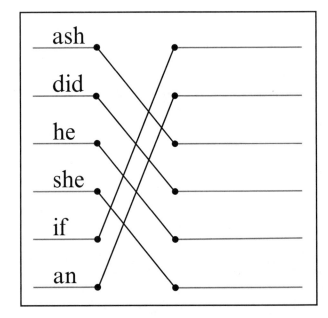

Name _____

Part 1

Follow the lines and copy each sound.

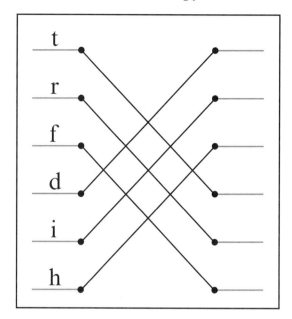

t

r

f

d

i

h

Part 2

Write in the missing letters.

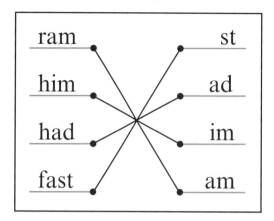

ram   st

him   ad

had   im

fast   am

Part 3

Draw lines to match the words and pictures.

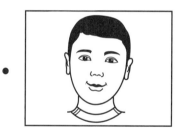

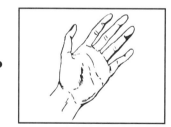

hand

he

she

Sound/symbol relationships, word completion, word recognition

Part 4

Circle the sounds.

(o) f o a f o s e t o s f a t o s h e f a s (8)
    o s t o s f t o s e i s f r f a o t e f r

(c) e f i p o c t o i c d f o i c f e f o d (8)
    h i c f o c i r c o i m c f i o a m c p e

(h) a h i n a h i a m s n e i n h a m o r (6)
    r m o s n o h a r o i h s i a n h i n r

Part 5

Follow the lines and copy each word.

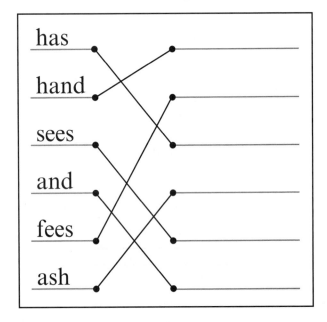

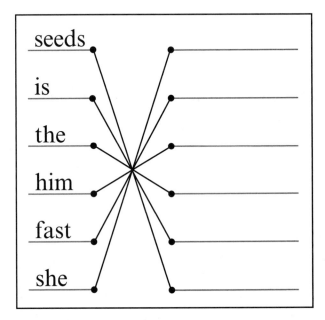

Sound/symbol relationships, copying words

Name _____

Part 1
Follow the lines and copy each sound.

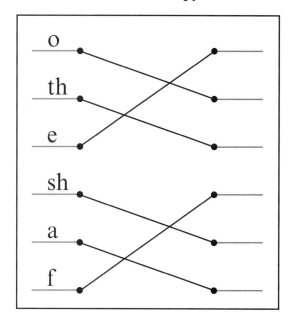

Part 2
Write in the missing letters.

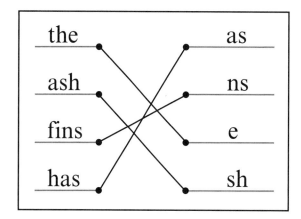

Part 3
Draw lines to match the words and pictures.

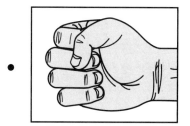

ram •

cast •

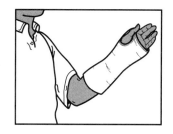

fist •

Sound/symbol relationships, word completion, word recognition

Name _____

Part 4

Circle the sounds.

(h) m e n t h m a n t h i n f d h o n f m e n (6)
h r n s m i n d h e m n f t m o n d h s n

(th) m e t h d n e f m t f i t h s h i h th f o (5)
e h th e f t o h f n a m th e n f m e d

(t) t h e l d m i a n d e i h f t n e d e f e r (6)
s m e n t h f d n e t m e t h d i a f t d f

Part 5

Follow the lines and copy each word.

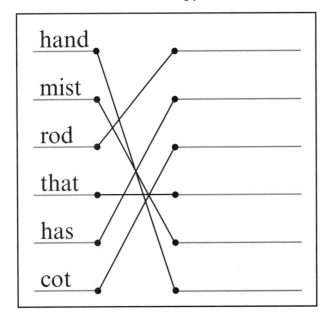

hand
mist
rod
that
has
cot

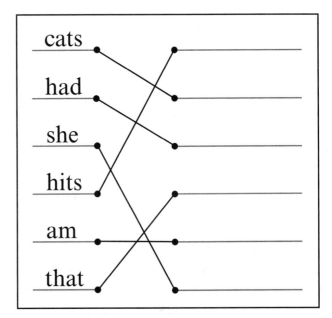

cats
had
she
hits
am
that

Sound/symbol relationships, copying words

Name _____

Part 1

Follow the lines and copy each sound.

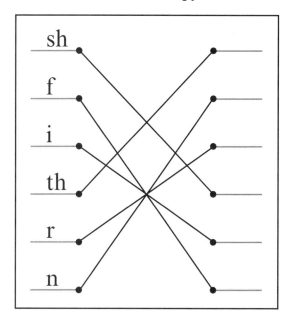

sh

f

i

th

r

n

Part 2

Write in the missing letters.

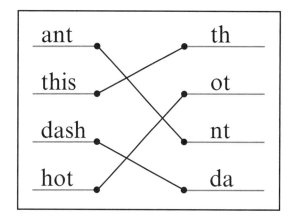

ant   th

this   ot

dash   nt

hot   da

Part 3

Draw lines to match the words and pictures.

ant

cans

man

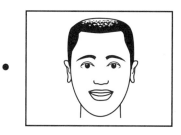

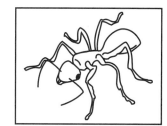

Sound/symbol relationships, word completion, word recognition

Lesson 20   **19**

Name _____

Part 4

Follow the lines and copy each word.

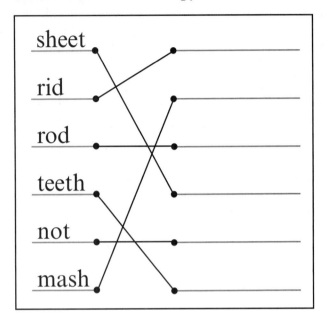

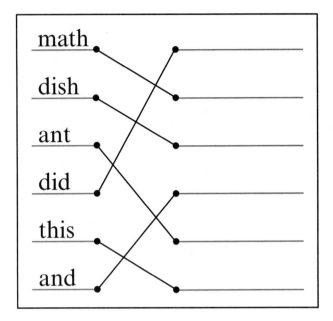

Part 5

Read the words.

ram	sheets	fast	dim
cast	she	fish	him
seeds	feet	did	cat
am	cats	fins	that

(Parent's/Listener's) signature _____ Date _____

Directions, Part 5:
1. Tell the student to read each row of words.
2. Make a check mark in the box if the student reads all the words in the row correctly.

Name _____

Part 1
Follow the lines and copy each sound.

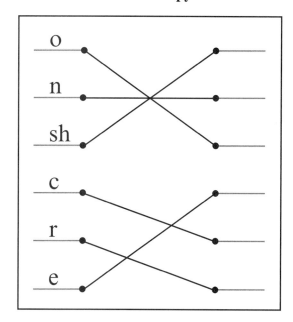

o

n

sh

c

r

e

Part 2
Write in the missing letters.

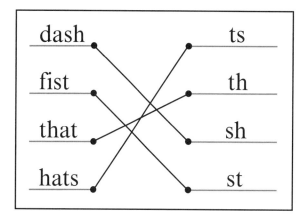

dash   ts

fist   th

that   sh

hats   st

Part 3
Draw lines to match the words and pictures.

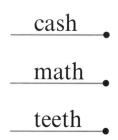

cash

math

teeth

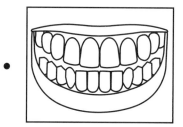

$$16 \quad 48$$
$$\times 5 \quad -12$$

Sound/symbol relationships, word completion, word recognition

Name _____

Part 4

Follow the lines and copy each word.

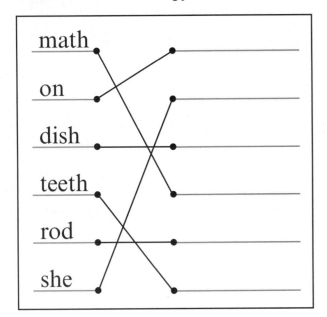

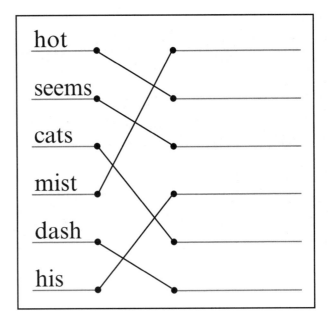

Part 5

Read the words.

hot	mist	can	and	☐
fist	not	cash	deed	☐
reef	tin	hand	cot	☐
fish	hat	ant	seeds	☐

(Parent's/Listener's) signature _____ Date _____

Directions, Part 5:
1. Tell the student to read each row of words.
2. Make a check mark in the box if the student reads all the words in the row correctly.

Part 1

Follow the lines and copy each sound.

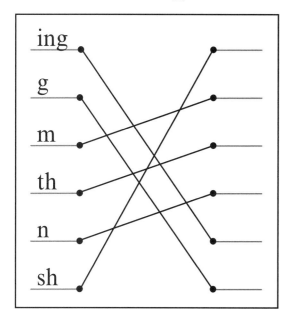

ing

g

m

th

n

sh

Part 2

Write in the missing letters.

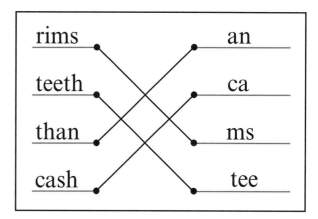

rims   an

teeth   ca

than   ms

cash   tee

Part 3

Circle the sounds.

(g)   t d f e g r i a t r f d g e a o i m n t h
     h a o i n t g h c s h m o f r i g a h t h   (7)
     r e i m o n f g s e i h r g f t d m i o g

(o)   m s t d f c s h o a e r i h t h n m e r f
     g o t c i m n r e o f s g h t i a c d o r   (6)
     a m n e o a r i s r d o g a r s i f t m t

(f)   d t r f e o g h i a f m n e o h g t r f e
     i o n c m f r t i s a g n e a m r f t h g   (7)
     n m c a d e s a f t i o m n a d f t h e t

(c)   a e f g c o i m n g f d e s a t r f g c i
     m n d f r e a s f c e d o i c a g r t s e   (6)
     n f g t c a t r i m n o t c o t d i n a m

Sound/symbol relationships, word completion

Name _____

Part 4

Follow the lines and copy each word.

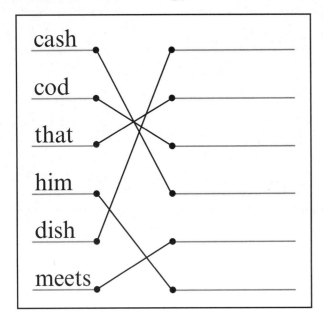

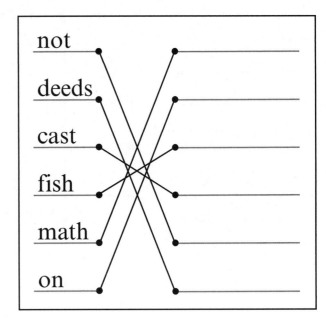

Part 5

Read the words.

hand	not	seems	sand
fast	is	mash	feed
dish	rod	sit	teeth
sheet	shad	math	on

(Parent's/Listener's) signature _____ Date _____

Directions, Part 5:
1. Tell the student to read each row of words.
2. Make a check mark in the box if the student reads all the words in the row correctly.

Name _____

Part 1

Follow the lines and copy each sound.

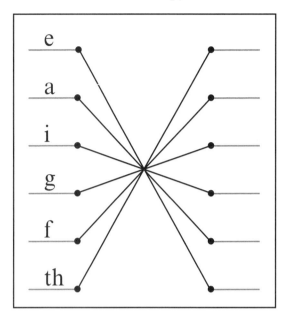

e

a

i

g

f

th

Part 2

Write in the missing letters.

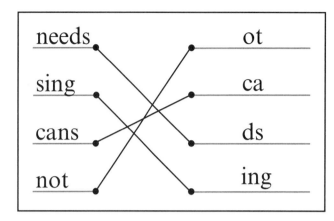

needs   ot

sing   ca

cans   ds

not   ing

Part 3

Draw lines to match the words and pictures.

hen

ant

he

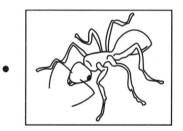

Sound/symbol relationships, word completion, word recognition

Part 4

Follow the lines and copy each word.

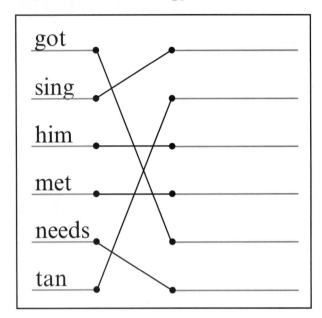

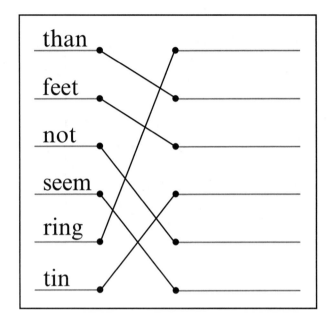

Part 5

Read the words.

cod	meet	ding	the	☐
feet	nod	sing	feed	☐
ring	seed	rod	than	☐
cash	she	me	not	☐

(Parent's/Listener's) signature _____ Date _____

Directions, Part 5:
1. Tell the student to read each row of words.
2. Make a check mark in the box if the student reads all the words in the row correctly.

Name _____

Part 1
Follow the lines and copy each sound.

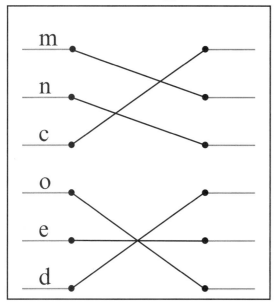

m
n
c
o
e
d

Part 2
Write in the missing letters.

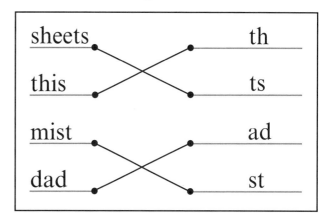

sheets   th
this   ts
mist   ad
dad   st

Part 3
Follow the lines and copy each word.

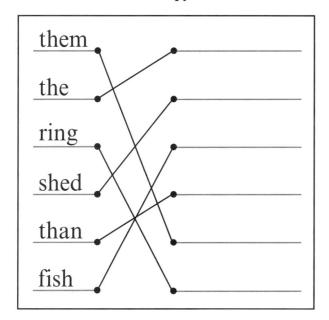

them
the
ring
shed
than
fish

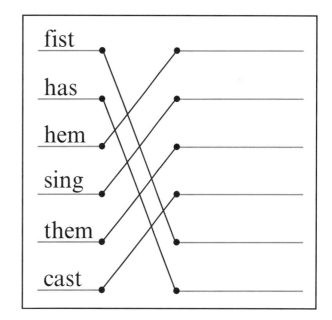

fist
has
hem
sing
them
cast

Sound/symbol relationships, word completion, copying words

Name _____

Part 4

Circle the sounds.

(n) m n r e n r m o a r t n s m t h s n i n m
  f t m e a t n e m s n t i h s e r t m o n ⑧

(sh) t h i s h e i f h s h e h f d t h s d t h
   t s h t e i f h s h e f s d f s h e t s h t ⑥

(th) s h e e t h f i g h e f t h i d r i m r
   t h r t d t e s n e t h f m e n t h s e ⑤

Part 5

Read the words and sentences.

them	sing	ant	fits	→ ☐
mash	not	thin	than	→ ☐
got	fast	seems	cot	→ ☐
teeth	his	sand	she	→ ☐

☐
☐

1. Dad did math.

2. She can see that reef.

(Parent's/Listener's) signature _____ Date _____

Directions, Part 5:
1. Tell the student to read each row of words and the sentences.
2. Make a check mark in the box if the student reads all the words in the row or in the sentence correctly.

Part 1

Write in the missing letters.

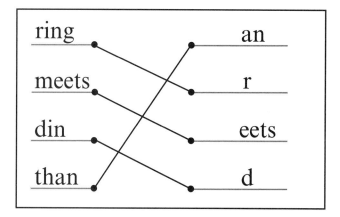

ring   an

meets   r

din   eets

than   d

Part 2

Follow the lines and copy each sound.

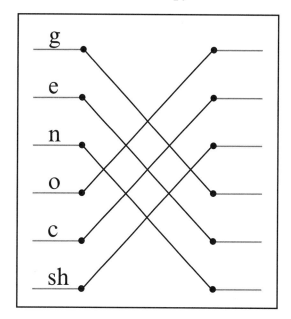

g

e

n

o

c

sh

Part 3

Follow the lines and copy each word.

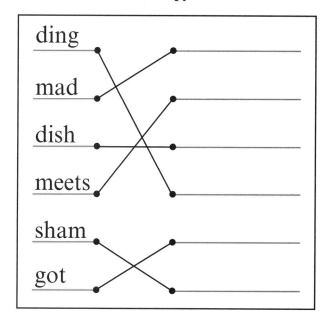

ding

mad

dish

meets

sham

got

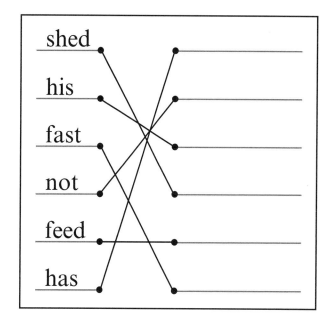

shed

his

fast

not

feed

has

Word completion, sound/symbol relationships, copying words

     Lesson 25   **29**

Name _____

Part 4
Circle the sounds.

(e) t d f e g r i a t r f d g e a o i m n th f   (5)
     a e i n t g h c sh m o f r i e a h t th e

(t) d t r f e o g h i a f m n e o h g t r f e   (4)
     i o n c m f r t i s a g n e a m r f t r g

(d) a e f g d c i m n g f d e s a t r f g c i   (5)
     d m n d f r e a s f c e d o i c a g r t s

(n) m s t d f n sh o a e r i h th n m e r f t   (4)
     o t c i m n r e o f g sh t th i a c d n r

Part 5
Read the words and sentences.

need	mad	fin	not	☐
ant	sing	feet	mist	☐
is	mod	has	if	☐
sand	than	shin	got	☐

☐
☐

1. That dash is fast.

2. He has rats and cats.

(Parent's/Listener's) signature _____ Date _____

Directions, Part 5:
1. Tell the student to read each row of words and the sentences.
2. Make a check mark in the box if the student reads all the words in the row or in the sentence correctly.

Name _____

Part 1

Follow the lines and copy each sound.

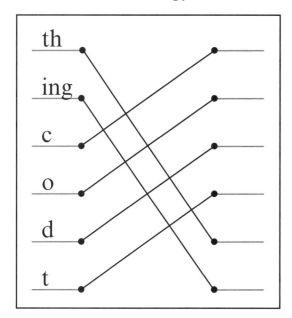

Part 2

Write in the missing letters.

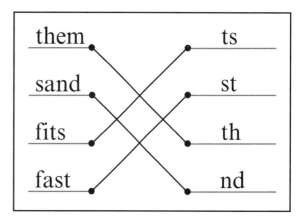

Part 3

Draw lines to match the words and pictures.

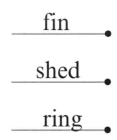

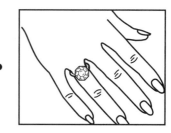

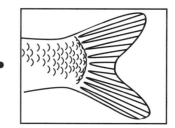

Sound/symbol relationships, word completion, word recognition

Name _____

Part 4
Follow the lines and copy each word.

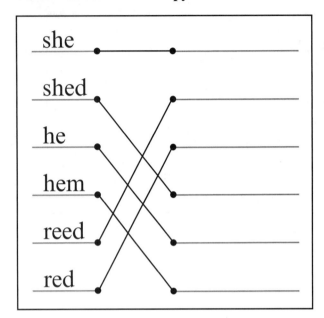

she _____ _____

shed _____ _____

he _____ _____

hem _____ _____

reed _____ _____

red _____ _____

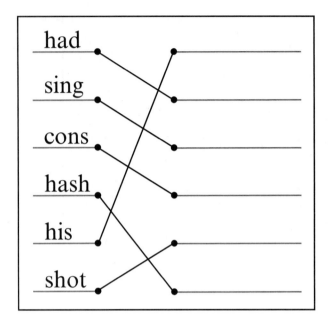

had _____ _____

sing _____ _____

cons _____ _____

hash _____ _____

his _____ _____

shot _____ _____

Part 5
Read the words and sentences.

and	cans	meet	sand	☐
fast	dish	rod	fits	☐
meet	hid	cash	hem	☐
sing	his	math	seems	☐

☐

☐

1. A cat had sand on his feet.

2. That fish has a fin.

(Parent's/Listener's) signature _____ Date _____

Directions, Part 5:
1. Tell the student to read each row of words and the sentences.
2. Make a check mark in the box if the student reads all the words in the row or in the sentence correctly.

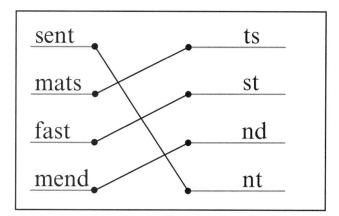

Lesson 27

Name _____

Part 1
Write in the missing letters.

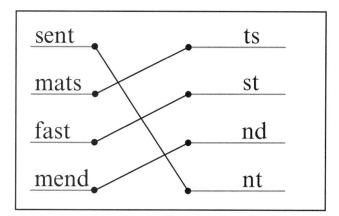

sent	ts
mats	st
fast	nd
mend	nt

Part 2
Follow the lines and copy each sound.

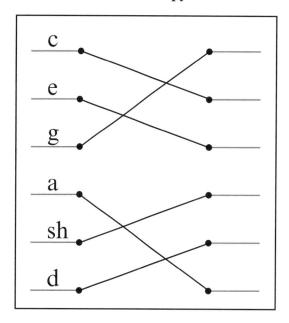

c
e
g
a
sh
d

Part 3
Follow the lines and copy each word.

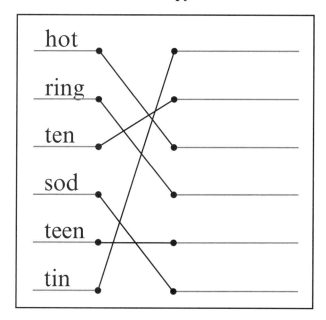

hot
ring
ten
sod
teen
tin

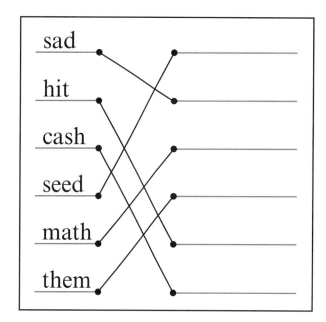

sad
hit
cash
seed
math
them

Word completion, sound/symbol relationships, copying words

Part 4
Circle the sounds.

(g) c d t f r i e a f t g c m a s r f c g r f h
     e a o c i m n g f t d f e g r i a t r f d g ⑤

(r) m n r a f e c g h i o a r e c d a s t f r
     o e a i n r m c e n o f r i s a h t th r e ⑥

(c) o a i c r f g h n m c e d r a s i o f g c
     e f r g i o c d e s a g n e c m r f t r g i ⑤

(e) d t r f e o g h i a f m n e o h g t r f e
     i o n c m f r t i s e d o i c a g r t s e m ⑤

Part 5
Read the words and sentences.

teen   ten   tan   tin   → ☐

end   send   mend   sand   → ☐

hit   hat   hot   that   → ☐

cash   dash   fast   dish   → ☐

1. She hid in the hen shed.   ☐

2. He met them on the ant hill.   ☐

(Parent's/Listener's) signature _____ Date _____

Directions, Part 5:
1. Tell the student to read each row of words and the sentences.
2. Make a check mark in the box if the student reads all the words in the row or in the sentence correctly.

Part 1

Follow the lines and copy each sound.

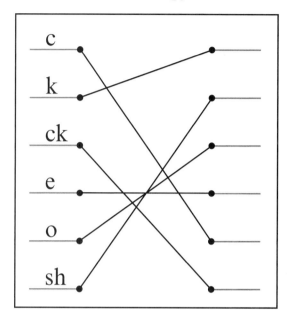

c

k

ck

e

o

sh

Part 2

Write in the missing letters.

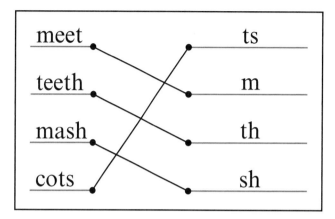

meet   ts

teeth   m

mash   th

cots   sh

Part 3

Draw lines to match the words and pictures.

ten

tent

teeth

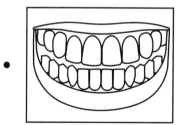

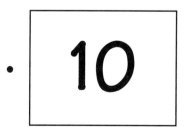

Sound/symbol relationships, word completion, word recognition

     Lesson 28   **35**

Name _____

Part 4
Follow the lines and copy each word.

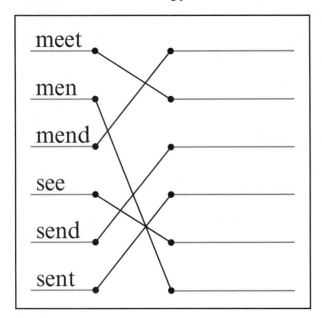

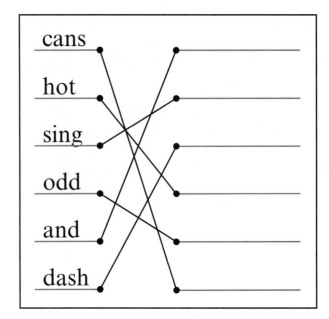

Part 5
Read the words and sentences.

sheets	shots	cots	cats	cash	→ ☐
mash	fish	fist	fast	mast	→ ☐
see	she	he	me	meet	→ ☐
nod	hat	hot	shot	sheet	→ ☐

1. Can she see if it is dim? ☐

2. He had cash in his hand. ☐

(Parent's/Listener's) signature _____ Date _____

Directions, Part 5:
1. Tell the student to read each row of words and the sentences.
2. Make a check mark in the box if the student reads all the words in the row or in the sentence correctly.

Part 1

Circle the sounds.

(k) g f t r d k s a r m n i o t h g r k o i r
    e d k s i o k n m d e f g h k i o m k n   (8)
    a r e t g h i o m n k d f g k o i r e m h

(h) d t r f e o g h i a f m n e o h g t r f a
    i o n c h f r t i s m s t d h c s o a h i   (8)
    h f n m e h f t g o t c i m n h e o i d e

(t) a g n e c m r f t r g i n m c a d t s a f
    t c m n a d h t f m n r a f t c g h i o a   (7)
    e c d a s t f g r o e a t i r m c e r h o

(i) a s d f i h k g o r e m n c d f g h k i o
    d a s m n c d f i e g h i k a e d r o e s   (7)
    n c r i s a o e d f r i o a i f g h t a m

Part 2

Write in the missing letters.

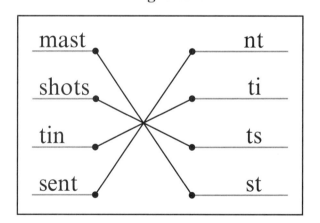

mast   nt

shots   ti

tin   ts

sent   st

Part 3

Follow the lines and copy each sound.

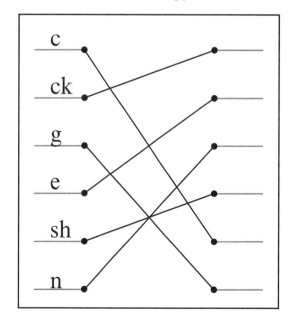

c

ck

g

e

sh

n

Sound/symbol relationships, word completion

Name _____

Part 4

Follow the lines and copy each word.

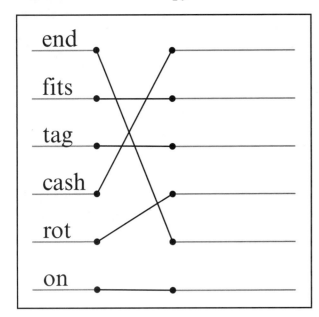

end _____

fits _____

tag _____

cash _____

rot _____

on _____

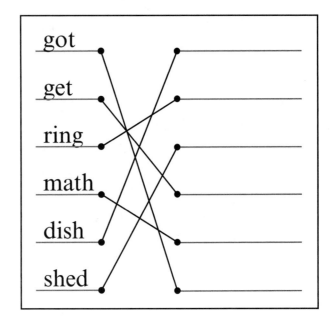

got _____

get _____

ring _____

math _____

dish _____

shed _____

Part 5

Read the words and sentences.

ten	hand	hot	tent	send	☐
sand	mist	mats	mend	mast	☐
fast	feed	got	red	get	☐
tin	sent	cans	tags	them	☐

☐
☐

1. Did she see the deed?

2. She got sand and ants in the dish.

(Parent's/Listener's) signature _____ Date _____

Directions, Part 5:
1. Tell the student to read each row of words and the sentences.
2. Make a check mark in the box if the student reads all the words in the row or in the sentence correctly.

Part 1

Follow the lines and copy each sound.

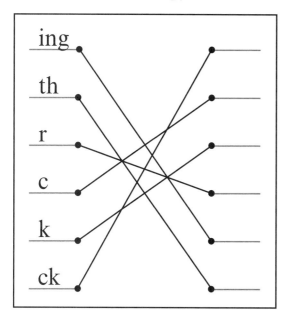

Part 2

Write in the missing letters.

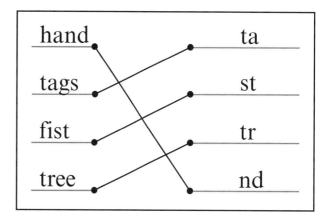

Part 3

Follow the lines and copy each word.

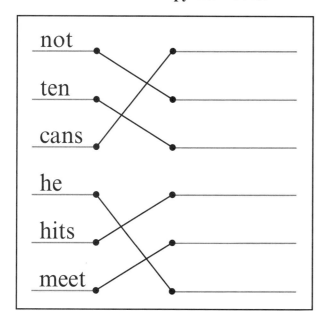

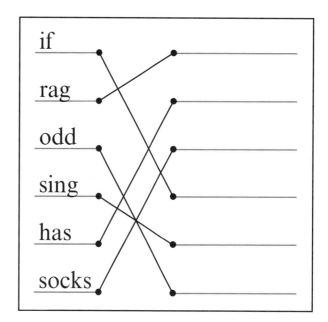

Sound/symbol relationships, word completion, copying words

Name _____

Part 4

Circle the sounds.

(d) s e m d c t a s m e d t s a c d e d
    a e d o m d e m s t f e d a h d f e   (8)

(g) m e i g a l c s g e m r s e g l o r
    g i l e g r e l s c e g r g e m h a   (7)

(ck) i t m ck e th i s e i d ck t e i ck e
     ck d e i t m ck i e th ck i e t th sh   (6)

Part 5

Read the words and sentences.

fig	add	get	tin	shots	
tent	cans	men	teeth	nod	
ant	hot	dash	his	fish	
leg	then	them	sacks	fits	

1. An ant is not fast in the dash.

2. Did he get mad at his cats?

(Parent's/Listener's) signature _____ Date _____

Directions, Part 5:
1. Tell the student to read each row of words and the sentences.
2. Make a check mark in the box if the student reads all the words in the row or in the sentence correctly.

Name _____

Part 1

Write in the missing letters.

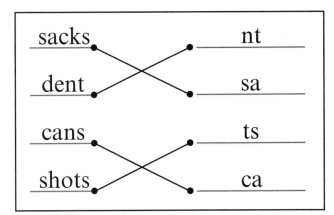

Part 2

Follow the lines and copy each sound.

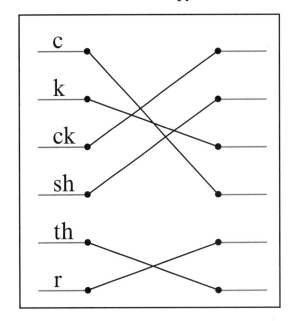

Part 3

Draw lines to match the words and pictures.

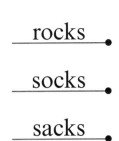

rocks •

socks •

sacks •

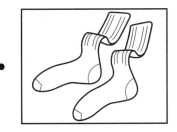

Word completion, sound/symbol relationships, word recognition

Name _____

Part 4

Follow the lines and copy each word.

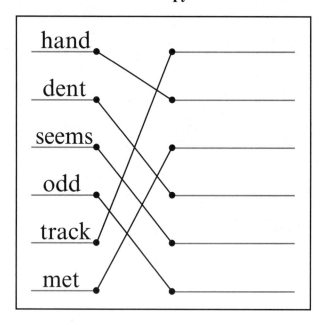

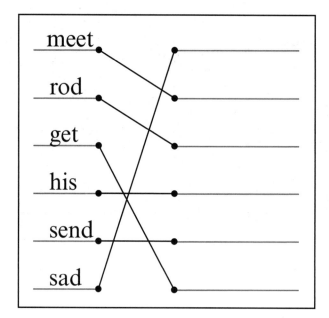

Part 5

Read the words and sentences.

then	sit	has	hid	feed	☐
fast	tree	trim	met	get	☐
kids	socks	cash	kick	this	☐
rags	shed	she	cod	sick	☐

☐

☐

1. Can she kick that sack?

2. He did his math as he sat on the mat.

(Parent's/Listener's) signature _____ Date _____

Directions, Part 5:
1. Tell the student to read each row of words and the sentences.
2. Make a check mark in the box if the student reads all the words in the row or in the sentence correctly.

Copying words, reading fluency

Part 1
Follow the lines and copy each sound.

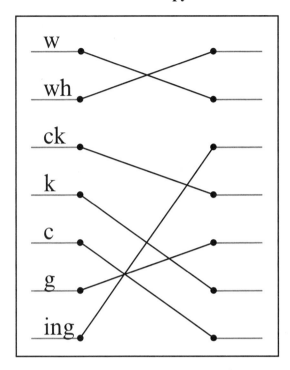

w	
wh	
ck	
k	
c	
g	
ing	

Part 2
Write in the missing letters.

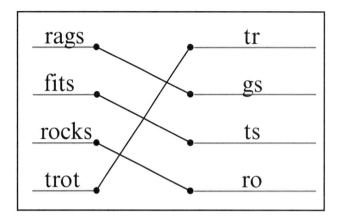

rags	tr
fits	gs
rocks	ts
trot	ro

Part 3
Draw lines to match the words and pictures.

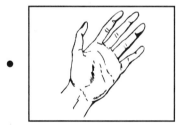

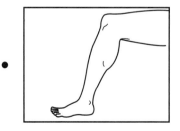

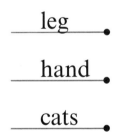

leg

hand

cats

Sound/symbol relationships, word completion, word recognition

Part 4

Follow the lines and copy each word.

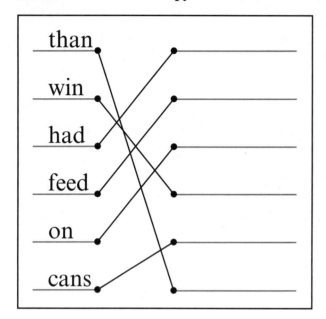
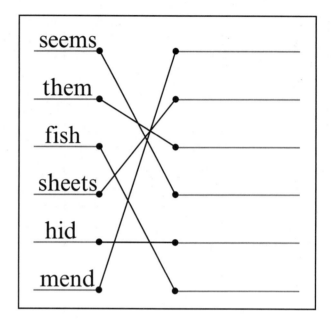

Part 5

Read the words and sentences.

did	dad	not	had	then
week	his	that	street	how
kicks	needs	ring	end	got
if	and	send	teen	rocks

1. Did she get a cast on the leg?

2. Can she sit and fish in the mist?

(Parent's/Listener's) signature _____ Date _____

Directions, Part 5:
1. Tell the student to read each row of words and the sentences.
2. Make a check mark in the box if the student reads all the words in the row or in the sentence correctly.

Part 1
Write in the missing letters.

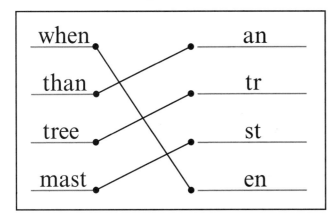

Part 2
Follow the lines and copy each sound.

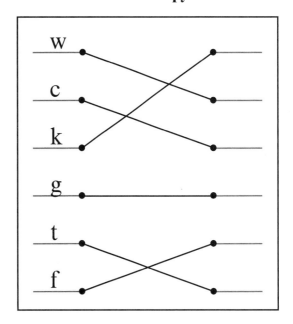

Part 3
Draw lines to match the words and pictures.

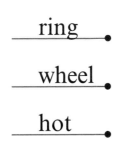

ring

wheel

hot

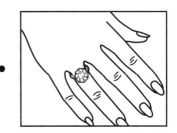

Word completion, sound/symbol relationships, word recognition

Name _____

Part 4

Follow the lines and copy each word.

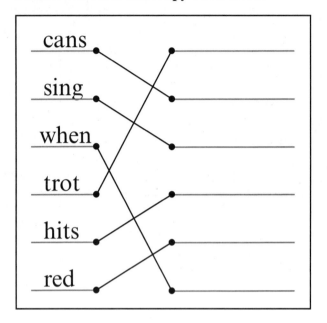

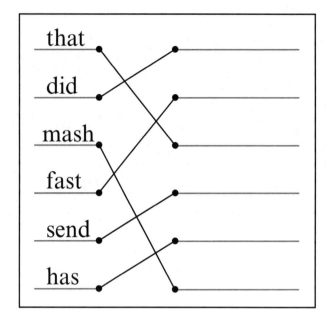

Part 5

Read the words and sentences.

we	when	wheel	with	this
sad	kick	dash	go	street
go	singing	tree	week	feed
sheets	shots	hot	how	hands

1. Did sand get in the street?

2. She did not see him.

(Parent's/Listener's) signature _____ Date _____

Directions, Part 5:
1. Tell the student to read each row of words and the sentences.
2. Make a check mark in the box if the student reads all the words in the row or in the sentence correctly.

Name _____

Part 1
Follow the lines and copy each sound.

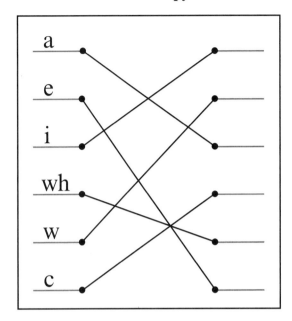

a

e

i

wh

w

c

Part 2
Write in the missing letters.

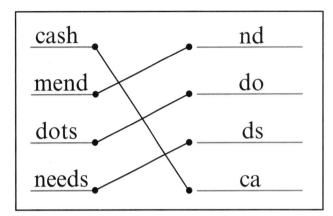

cash

mend

dots

needs

nd

do

ds

ca

Part 3
Draw lines to match the words and pictures.

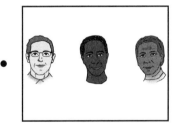

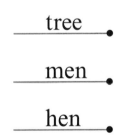

tree

men

hen

Sound/symbol relationships, word completion, word recognition

Name _____

Part 4
Circle the words.

(his) a t i f o n i n h i s h a s m e e t r e s e e h i s n o t h i s t h e d i s h
f i s h a n d n o d h i s o d d t h e n w h e n h i s m a t h c o d h i s f ⑥

(at) h i t s h e r o c k a t m e t r i n g o o n a t a m h e m e s e e m a t i n
m a d s i t a t s o c k h i s m a s h a t f a s t w i t h a t s e e w i n a t ⑦

(miss) m a s s r e e m s e e m s s a m m i s s m i t t f e e d r i m s m i s s r
m e e t m i s s m a s s r e e m m a s t m i s s m i s t m e f e e t m i s s ⑤

Part 5
Read the words and sentences.

no	not	got	go	get	□
had	hand	sent	cans	cast	□
trot	tree	street	wheel	we	□
ring	ringing	with	math	mash	□

1. Can she see when it is dim?   □

2. His fat fish is not fast.   □

(Parent's/Listener's) signature _____ Date _____

Directions, Part 5:
1. Tell the student to read each row of words and the sentences.
2. Make a check mark in the box if the student reads all the words in the row or in the sentence correctly.

Part 1

Write in the missing letters.

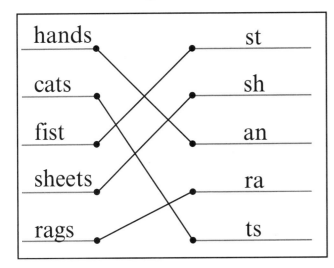

hands	st
cats	sh
fist	an
sheets	ra
rags	ts

Part 2

Follow the lines and copy each sound.

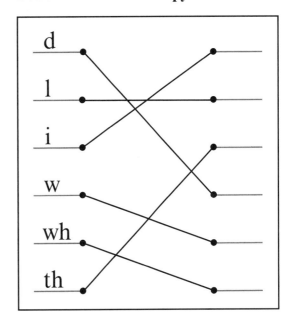

d

l

i

w

wh

th

Part 3

Circle the words.

(met) a t h e m e s e e m e t m a d r a m e e t m e t w e t s a m s e m e t s
s h e m e t m i s s r e e m s a c k m e t m i s s c a m s c a s t m e t s ⑥

(on) i n a s a m r a m o n i n i s h o t r o d o n g o t g e t i t i n o n i f i s
g o f a s t i f o n h o t g e t o n i s a s a m m a d o n i f i n o n m e e ⑦

(sad) s e e d s i d s e e m s a d s i c k h a d m a d s a d r i d r o d h i d h a
m a d o n i f s a d s a c k s e e m r e e f a s a m s a d s o c k s o s a d ⑤

Word completion, sound/symbol relationships, word matching

Part 4

Follow the lines and copy each word.

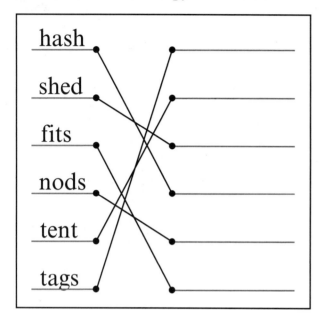

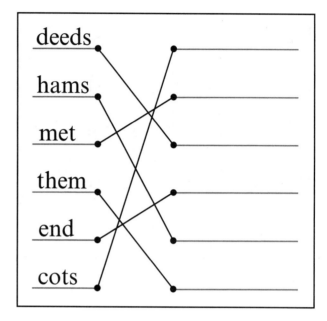

Part 5

Read the words and sentences.

dash	dish	fish	fist	fast	→ ☐
cast	cot	hot	how	rods	→ ☐
we	win	with	math	then	→ ☐
when	wheel	rocks	sheets	rag	→ ☐

☐

1. She is sad and sick.

☐

2. When did the man feed his cats?

(Parent's/Listener's) signature _____ Date _____

Directions, Part 5:
1. Tell the student to read each row of words and the sentences.
2. Make a check mark in the box if the student reads all the words in the row or in the sentence correctly.

Lesson 36

Name _____

Part 1
Follow the lines and copy each sound.

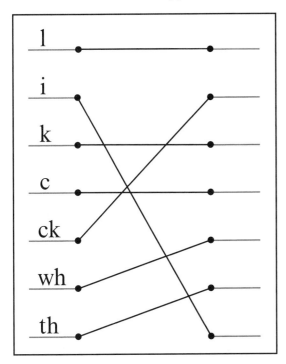

l

i

k

c

ck

wh

th

Part 2
Write in the missing letters.

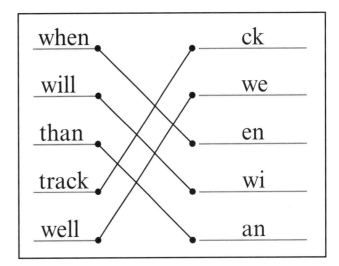

when   ck

will   we

than   en

track   wi

well   an

Part 3
Draw lines to match the words and pictures.

sick

sock

lock

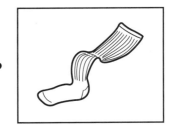

Sound/symbol relationships, word completion, word recognition

Lesson 36   **51**

Part 4

Follow the lines and copy each word.

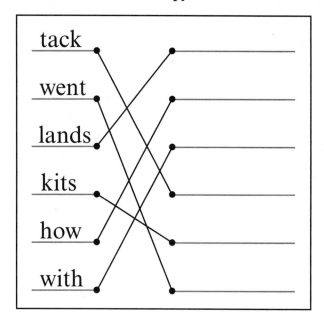

tack _____

went _____

lands _____

kits _____

how _____

with _____

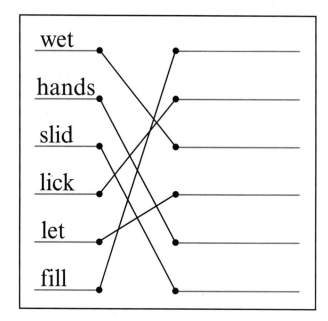

wet _____

hands _____

slid _____

lick _____

let _____

fill _____

Part 5

Read the words and sentences.

trot	trick	track	lack	lock	☐
fill	will	well	fell	feet	☐
sand	send	sent	when	wheel	☐
not	now	how	hot	hats	☐

☐

☐

1. She got wet in the street.

2. When he sings, I get sad.

(Parent's/Listener's) signature _____ Date _____

Directions, Part 5:
1. Tell the student to read each row of words and the sentences.
2. Make a check mark in the box if the student reads all the words in the row or in the sentence correctly.

Part 1
Write in the missing letters.

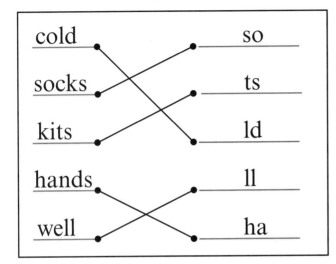

cold	so
socks	ts
kits	ld
hands	ll
well	ha

Part 2
Follow the lines and copy each sound.

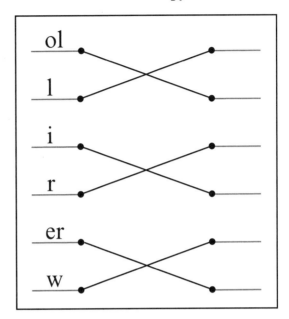

ol
l
i
r
er
w

Part 3
Circle the words.

(it) i s i n o n i t a n t t h a t s e e m i t i f i s o n h e h a s i t f a s t o n i t i ⑦
n o t n o d t h e i t i n i s o n w e t g o t f i n w i n i t i f o n t r i m i t f i

(the) t h a t t h a n t h e t h i s t h e t h a n t r e e t e e a g s t h e a t t h e a t ⑧
t r a c k t h e t h a t t r i c k t h e t h i s t a c k t h e t a n t h e t e n t h

(fit) f i s t f a s t f i n s f i t f i g s f i s h f i l l f i t f i s t f a t f i t f a s t f i ⑦
s h f i t f i n f e l l f i t f i n f a n f a s t f i t f i s t f i l l f i n f i t f a s t

Word completion, sound/symbol relationships, word matching

Part 4

Follow the lines and copy each word.

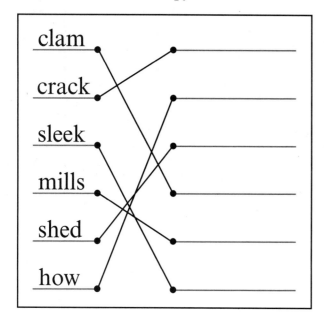

clam
crack
sleek
mills
shed
how

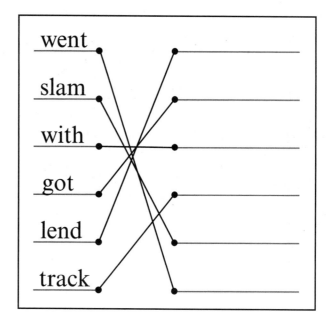

went
slam
with
got
lend
track

Part 5

Read the words and sentences.

get	got	rags	gas	cats	☐
trim	trees	street	send	hands	☐
sacks	lick	click	lack	lands	☐
wet	went	will	wheel	when	☐

1. That wheel has wet sand on it.

2. I did not see that shell.

☐
☐

(Parent's/Listener's) signature _____ Date _____

Name _____

Part 1
Follow the lines and copy each sound.

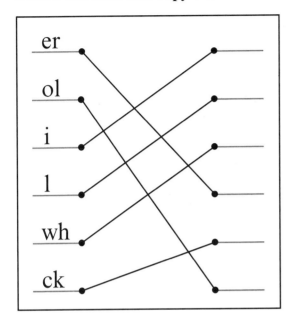

er
ol
i
l
wh
ck

Part 2
Write in the missing letters.

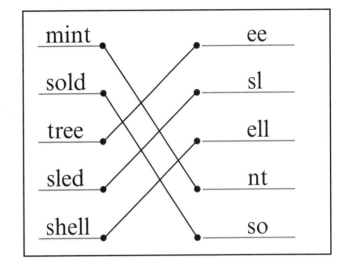

mint   ee
sold   sl
tree   ell
sled   nt
shell   so

Part 3
Circle the sentence that tells about the picture.

This wheel has a track in it.

This wheel has a tack in it.

This wheel has a rack on it.

Directions, Part 3: Read the directions to the student: *Circle the sentence that tells about the picture.*

Part 4

Follow the lines and copy each word.

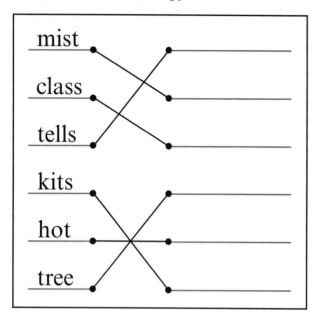

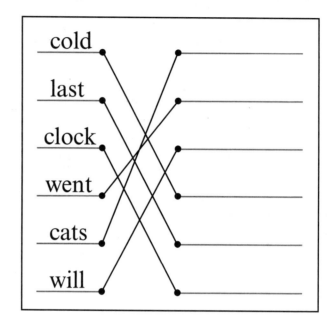

Part 5

Read the words and sentences.

cold	sold	sled	slam	land	☐
lend	lack	cracks	shack	shell	☐
street	sell	tells	slim	hill	☐
has	hold	how	her	letter	☐

1. Ten cats did not feel well. ☐

2. She slid her sled on the hill. ☐

(Parent's/Listener's) signature _____ Date _____

Directions, Part 5:
1. Tell the student to read each row of words and the sentences.
2. Make a check mark in the box if the student reads all the words in the row or in the sentence correctly.

Part 1

Write in the missing letters.

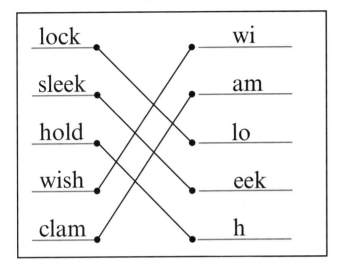

lock	wi___
sleek	___am
hold	___lo
wish	___eek
clam	___h

Part 2

Follow the lines and copy each sound.

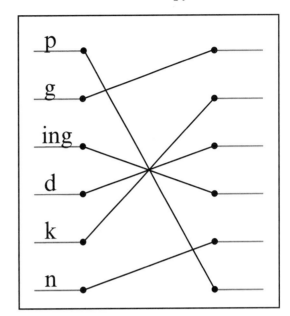

p

g

ing

d

k

n

Part 3

Circle the sentence that tells about the picture.

He has a cat in his hand.

He has a rat in his hand.

He has an ant in his hand.

Word completion, sound/symbol relationships, sentence reading

Name _____

Part 4

Follow the lines and copy each word.

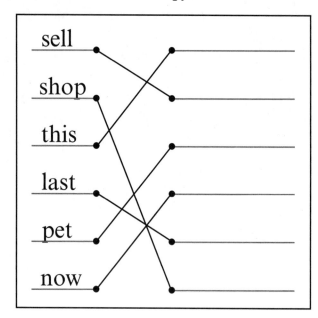

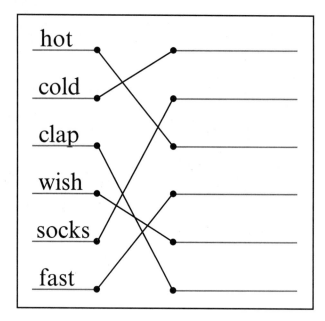

Part 5

Read the words and sentences.

this	than	then	when	well	□
fell	tells	sad	sadder	how	□
will	win	winner	lip	slip	□
last	list	land	pet	pit	□

□

□

1. How well can she sing?

2. If it is not hot, we will sleep.

(Parent's/Listener's) signature _____ Date _____

Directions, Part 5:
1. Tell the student to read each row of words and the sentences.
2. Make a check mark in the box if the student reads all the words in the row or in the sentence correctly.

Name _____

Part 1
Follow the lines and copy each sound.

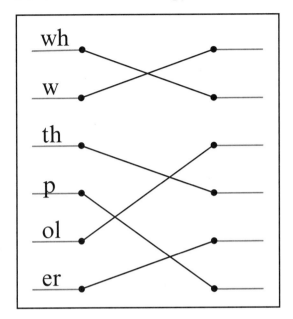

wh

w

th

p

ol

er

Part 2
Write in the missing letters.

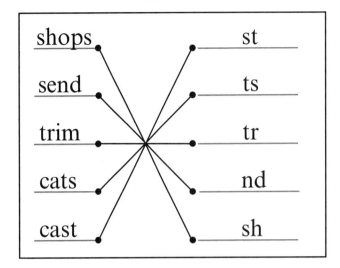

shops	st
send	ts
trim	tr
cats	nd
cast	sh

Part 3
Draw lines to match the words and pictures.

pig

flag

clock

Sound/symbol relationships, word completion, word recognition

Name _____

Part 4

Follow the lines and copy each word.

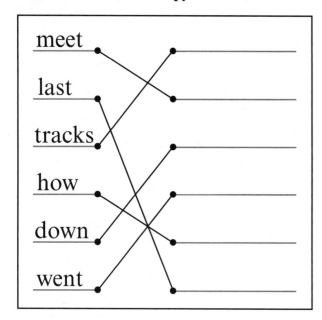

meet
last
tracks
how
down
went

_____
_____
_____
_____
_____
_____

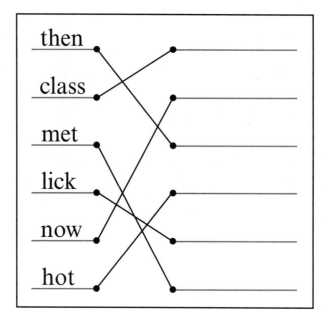

then
class
met
lick
now
hot

_____
_____
_____
_____
_____
_____

Part 5

Read the words and sentences.

pig	pet	petting	pack	tack	→	☐
sing	singer	letter	think	how	→	☐
has	hats	hand	lands	lend	→	☐
lip	slip	sleep	sheep	tree	→	☐

1. That cat is slim and sleek.   ☐

2. How fast can he go with that cast?   ☐

(Parent's/Listener's) signature _____ Date _____

Directions, Part 5:
1. Tell the student to read each row of words and the sentences.
2. Make a check mark in the box if the student reads all the words in the row or in the sentence correctly.

Name _____

Part 1
Write in the missing letters.

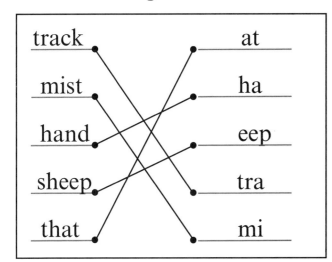

track	at
mist	ha
hand	eep
sheep	tra
that	mi

Part 2
Follow the lines and copy each sound.

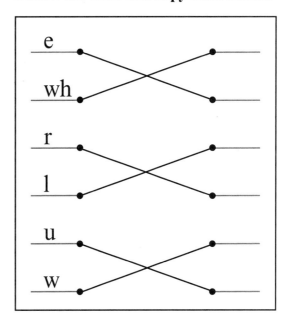

e

wh

r

l

u

w

Part 3
Circle the words.

(and) s e n d s l a m a n d w i l l a m a n a n t a n a n d f a n f i n a n d f i
a n t a m i n o n s a m a n d s e n d a n t a n d c a n a n d h a m a n t ⑥

(well) s e l l n t w i l l w e l l f e l l t e l l s w e l l f i l l c l i c k w e l l s e
h i l l f i l l w e l l f e l l w i l l w h e e l w h e n w e l l t e l l s e l l ⑤

(hat) h a s h a d h e s h e h a t t h a n h a t h o t h i t s h e d h o t h a t h
a m h a t h e h a s h h a m s a n d h a t h a m h i s h a t h e e d h o ⑥

Word completion, sound/symbol relationships, word matching

Lesson 41 **61**

Name _____

Part 4

Follow the lines and copy each word.

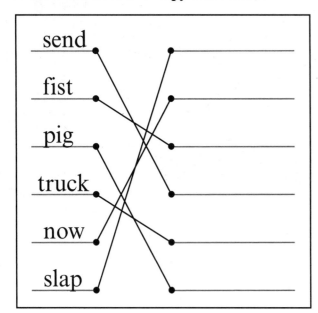

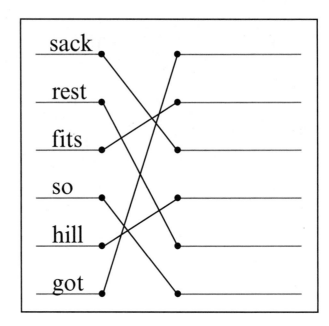

Part 5

Read the words and sentences.

list	last	mast	pit	pet	☐
peek	sleek	sleep	lip	slip	☐
not	now	how	hash	cast	☐
fill	filler	trap	clock	dents	☐

1. Will he mend his socks? ☐

2. Her dad has a hat that fits. ☐

(Parent's/Listener's) signature _____ Date _____

Directions, Part 5:
1. Tell the student to read each row of words and the sentences.
2. Make a check mark in the box if the student reads all the words in the row or in the sentence correctly.

Part 1

Follow the lines and copy each sound.

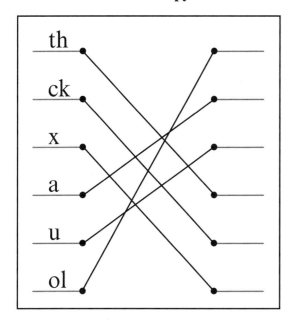

th
ck
x
a
u
ol

Part 2

Write in the missing letters.

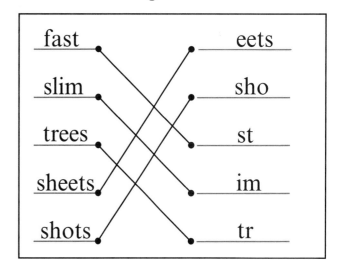

fast   eets
slim   sho
trees   st
sheets   im
shots   tr

Part 3

Circle the sentence that tells about the picture.

Her hand is on her pet pig.

The hat is on her pet pig.

Her pet pig is on the hat.

Sound/symbol relationships, word completion, sentence reading

Part 4

Follow the lines and copy each word.

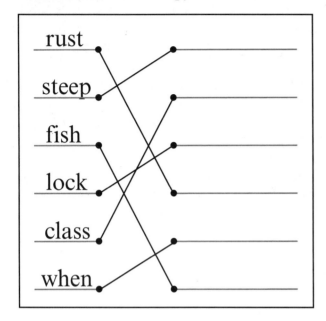

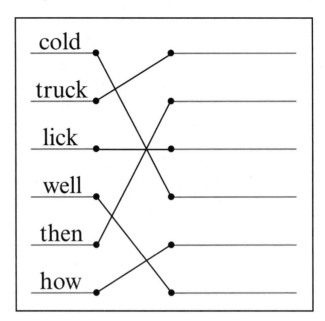

Part 5

Read the words and sentences.

send	sender	sending	rest	last

fold	up	under	stop	truck

step	stem	sleds	clam	crash

fins	fishing	mud	pots	dug

1. I sent her a clock last week.

2. That singer will sing at the dinner.

3. The winner got a gold ring.

(Parent's/Listener's) signature _____ Date _____

Directions, Part 5:
1. Tell the student to read each row of words and the sentences.
2. Make a check mark in the box if the student reads all the words in the row or in the sentence correctly.

Part 1
Write in the missing letters.

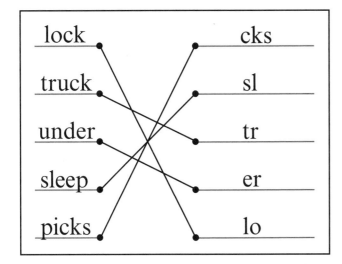

lock	cks
truck	sl
under	tr
sleep	er
picks	lo

Part 2
Follow the lines and copy each sound.

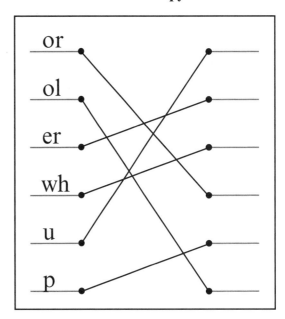

or
ol
er
wh
u
p

Part 3
Circle the sentence that tells about the picture.

She has a lock in her hand.

She has a cast on her hand.

She has a clock in her hand.

Word completion, sound/symbol relationships, sentence reading

Part 4

Follow the lines and copy each word.

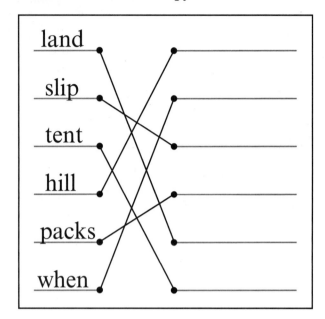

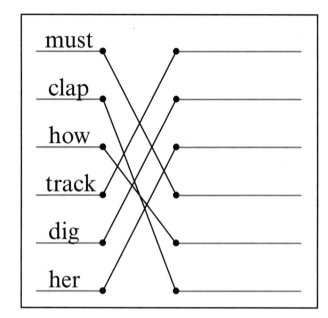

Part 5

Read the words and sentences.

rocks	rocking	locks	list	lip	☐
went	win	winning	sending	sand	☐
slap	clap	click	trick	tracks	☐
ran	run	sings	thing	this	☐

☐

☐

1. Meet me on the hill. ☐

2. He has a cast on his leg. ☐

3. How will we get dinner on this ship?

(Parent's/Listener's) signature _____ Date _____

Directions, Part 5:
1. Tell the student to read each row of words and the sentences.
2. Make a check mark in the box if the student reads all the words in the row or in the sentence correctly.

Name _____

Part 1

Follow the lines and copy each sound.

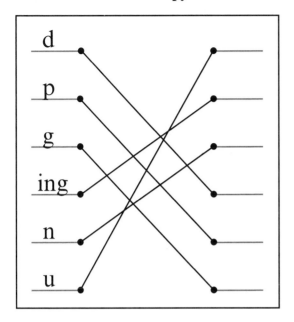

d

p

g

ing

n

u

Part 2

Write in the missing letters.

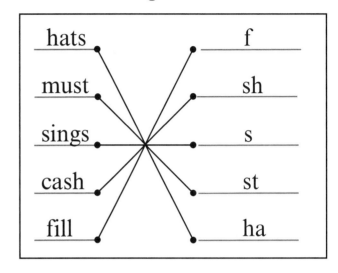

hats   f

must   sh

sings   s

cash   st

fill   ha

Part 3

Circle the words.

(then) w h e n w i l l w e n t t h i s t h e n w e e k s l e e k t h a t t h e n t h i ④
        w e l l w h e n t h e n t h a t w h e e l t h e n t h i s t h a t t h e w h e n

(not)   n o w h o w h o t n o t s t o p s o c k n o t t t h a n t a n n e e d n o t s ⑥
        o n i t h o t n o t p o t s n o g o n o t h o t r o t r o d h o w n o t n o w

(fast) c a s h f i s h f a s t m a s t f i s t m a s h m i s t f a s t c a s t c a n ④
        f i n s f i g s f a d d a s h f a s t c a s t m i s t f i s h f e l l f a s t f

Sound/symbol relationships, word completion, word matching

Part 4

Follow the lines and copy each word.

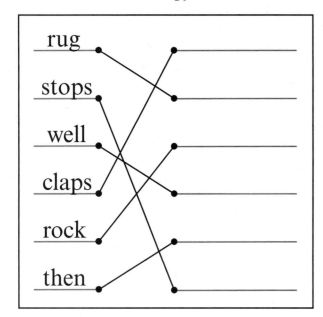

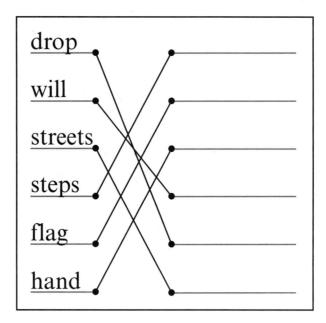

Part 5

Read the words and sentences.

run	fun	fox	fix	fold	☐
dinner	sadder	letter	pens	runs	☐
week	sings	sleep	slip	sun	☐
mist	must	get	got	dot	☐

1. Send me the clock this week. ☐

2. No man will rent that shack. ☐

3. Stop filling that gas can with sand. ☐

(Parent's/Listener's) signature _____ Date _____

Directions, Part 5:
1. Tell the student to read each row of words and the sentences.
2. Make a check mark in the box if the student reads all the words in the row or in the sentence correctly.

Name _____

Part 1

Write in the missing letters.

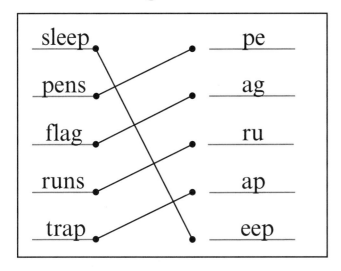

sleep	pe ___
pens	ag ___
flag	ru ___
runs	ap ___
trap	eep ___

Part 2

Follow the lines and copy each sound.

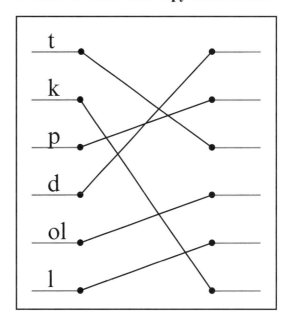

t

k

p

d

ol

l

Part 3

Circle the sentence that tells about the picture.

The cat sat on the truck.

The fish sat on the truck.

The cat sat on the fish.

Word completion, sound/symbol relationships, sentence reading

Part 4

Follow the lines and copy each word.

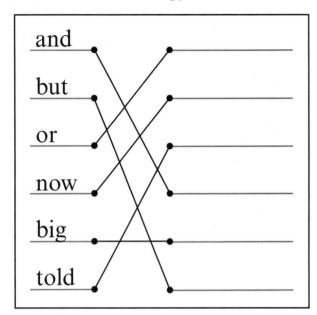

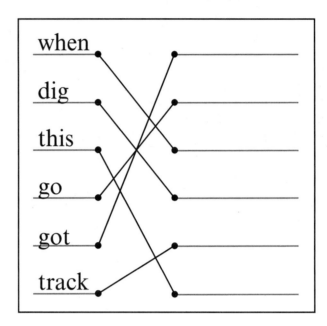

Part 5

Read the words and sentences.

clap	claps	clapping	street	picks	☐
or	form	torn	must	fell	☐
but	bug	big	dig	dug	☐
pins	peel	told	tag	flags	☐

1. The old man fell on the dock and got wet. ☐

2. She will sing for the class. ☐

3. His socks fit, but his hat is big. ☐

(Parent's/Listener's) signature _____ Date _____

Directions, Part 5:
1. Tell the student to read each row of words and the sentences.
2. Make a check mark in the box if the student reads all the words in the row or in the sentence correctly.

Name _____

Part 1
Follow the lines and copy each sound.

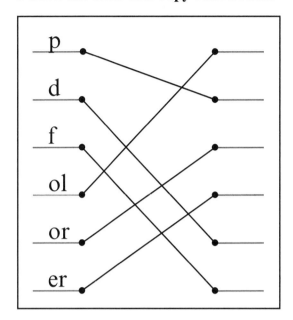

p
d
f
ol
or
er

Part 2
Write in the missing letters.

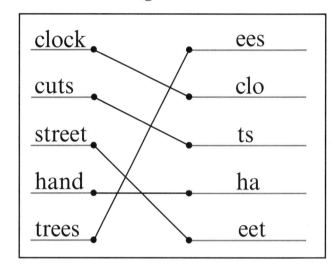

clock · · ees
cuts · · clo
street · · ts
hand · · ha
trees · · eet

Part 3
Draw lines to match the words and pictures.

fins ·

rams ·

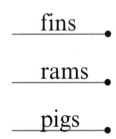

pigs ·

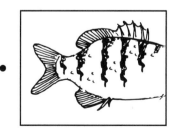

Sound/symbol relationships, word completion, word recognition

Part 4

Follow the lines and copy each word.

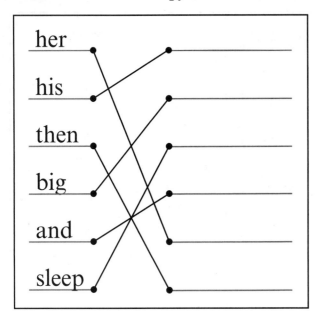

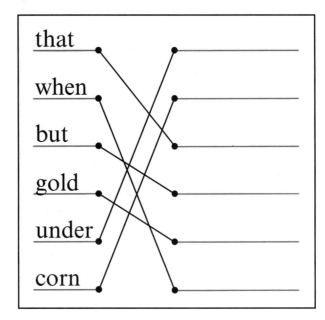

Part 5

Read the words and sentences.

rip	trip	grip	with	went	☐
dents	dig	bug	bust	dust	☐
how	now	no	so	sold	☐
pin	pinning	sends	winner	winning	☐

1. She is trim and fast.   ☐

2. I am a big winner.   ☐

3. We will clap if she sings well.   ☐

(Parent's/Listener's) signature _____ Date _____

Directions, Part 5:
1. Tell the student to read each row of words and the sentences.
2. Make a check mark in the box if the student reads all the words in the row or in the sentence correctly.

Part 1
Write in the missing letters.

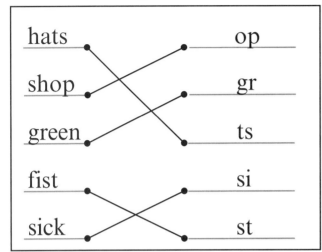

hats
shop
green
fist
sick

op
gr
ts
si
st

Part 2
Follow the lines and copy each sound.

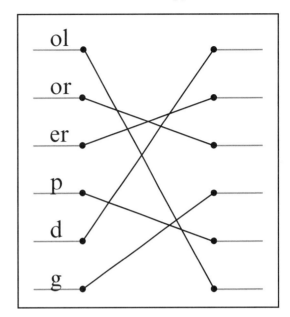

ol
or
er
p
d
g

Part 3
Circle the sentence that tells about the picture.

He ran down the steep hill.

He fell down the steep hill.

He ran up the steep hill.

Part 4

Follow the lines and copy each word.

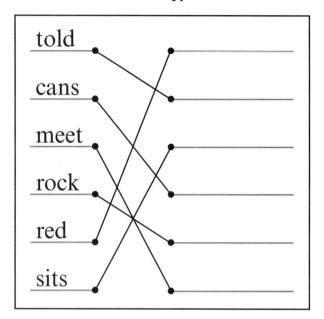

told

cans

meet

rock

red

sits

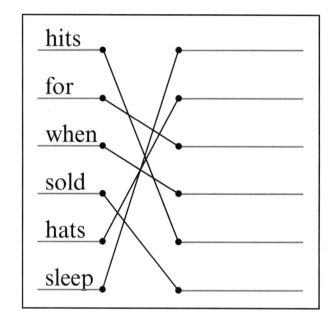

hits

for

when

sold

hats

sleep

Part 5

Read the words and sentences.

corn	born	big	bug	dust	☐
send	sender	finger	pins	pinning	☐
sold	fold	for	horn	how	☐
slip	sheep	shops	stop	swim	☐

1. He will lend us his tent. ☐

2. She had dinner with us last week. ☐

3. When did the bell ring? ☐

(Parent's/Listener's) signature _____ Date _____

Directions, Part 5:
1. Tell the student to read each row of words and the sentences.
2. Make a check mark in the box if the student reads all the words in the row or in the sentence correctly.

Name _____

Part 1
Follow the lines and copy each sound.

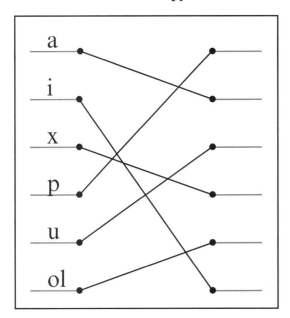

a

i

x

p

u

ol

Part 2
Draw the lines. Then write in the missing letters.

big .	. ___ eep
must .	. ___ b
sleep .	. ___ us
track .	. ___ nt
went .	. ___ ac

Part 3
Circle the words.

(end)   h a n d a n d l e n d s a n d s e n d p e n s m e n d f a n s h a m s a n
s l e d p e n s p a n s e n d s h e d c a n s e n d h a n d s s l e d e n d   ⑥

(his)   t h a t t h e t h e n h i s h a m h i t s h a m t h e t h e n h i s h i m h
h o w h i t h i s h i l l s h i n h i s w i t h a t w i l l h i s h i m h e h i   ⑤

(stop)   s t e p s t e e p s t r e e t s t o p p o p s t e p s l i p s t o p s l i d s l e
e k p o t s t o p s l p o p s t o p s l e d s l e e k s t o p s t e p s p o t s   ⑤

(when)   w e t e n d w h e e l w e e k w h e n t h a t t h e n w e l l w h e n w i
t h e n w h e n t h a t w e n t w i l l w h e n w i n w h e n w h e e l h   ⑤

Directions, Part 2: Read the directions to the student: *Draw the lines. Then write in the missing letters.*

Lesson 48   **75**

Part 4

Follow the lines and copy each word.

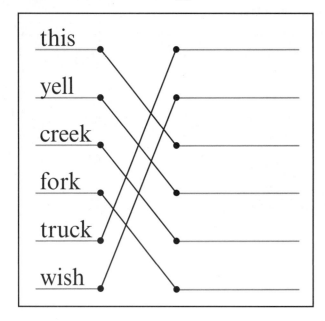

this _____

yell _____

creek _____

fork _____

truck _____

wish _____

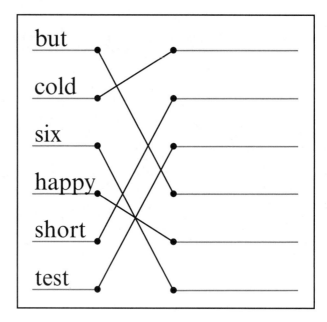

but _____

cold _____

six _____

happy _____

short _____

test _____

Part 5

Read the words and sentences.

lack	slack	truck	rugs	crust	☐
slip	fix	shed	silly	happy	☐
yes	bell	bet	fist	land	☐
mix	fox	fits	sold	short	☐

☐

1. Is she swimming in the pond?
☐

2. The fox is running up the steep hill.
☐

3. That black colt will trot on the track.

(Parent's/Listener's) signature _____ Date _____

Directions, Part 5:
1. Tell the student to read each row of words and the sentences.
2. Make a check mark in the box if the student reads all the words in the row or in the sentence correctly.

Part 1

Draw the lines. Then write in the missing letters.

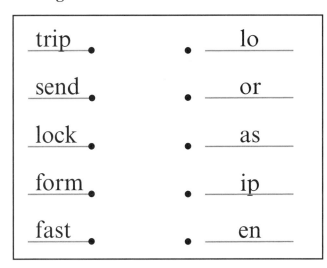

trip	lo
send	or
lock	as
form	ip
fast	en

Part 2

Follow the lines and copy each sound.

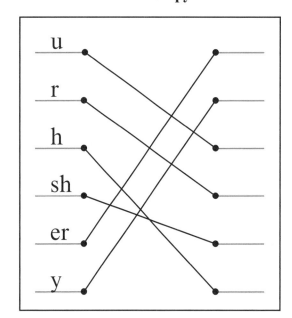

u
r
h
sh
er
y

Part 3

Draw lines to match the words and pictures.

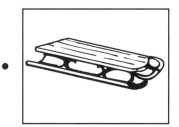

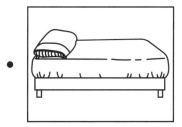

bed

sled

tent

Word completion, sound/symbol relationships, word recognition

Name _____

Part 4

Follow the lines and copy each word.

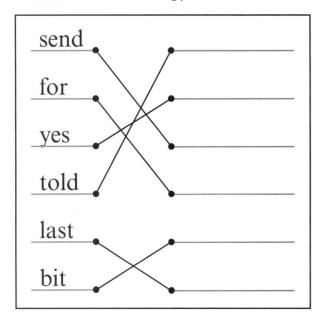

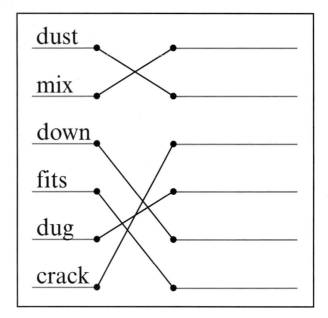

Part 5

Read the words and sentences.

cold	creek	fork	fun	funny	☐
letter	lasting	better	drip	pit	☐
rush	dust	brush	bits	gift	☐
swim	rub	running	flags	sleep	☐

☐

1. The class will end with a test. ☐

2. When can we swim in the creek? ☐

3. His cat is sleeping in his bed. ☐

(Parent's/Listener's) signature _____ Date _____

Directions, Part 5:
1. Tell the student to read each row of words and the sentences.
2. Make a check mark in the box if the student reads all the words in the row or in the sentence correctly.

Part 1
Follow the lines and copy each sound.

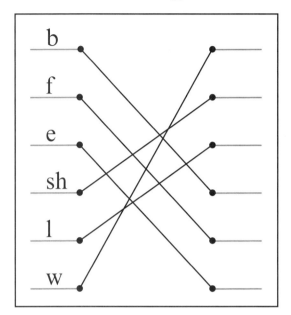

b

f

e

sh

l

w

Part 2
Draw the lines. Then write in the missing letters.

born .   . ac ___

slip .   . mi ___

dug .   . or ___

sack .   . ip ___

mist .   . u ___

Part 3
Circle the sentence that tells about the picture.

She can not sleep in the short tent.

She can not fit in the short truck.

She can sleep on the short bed.

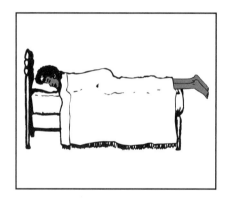

Sound/symbol relationships, word completion, sentence reading

Name _____

Part 4
Follow the lines and copy each word.

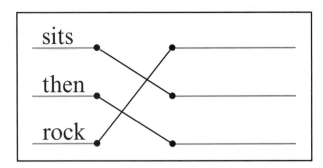

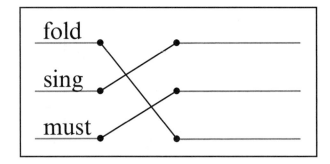

Part 5
Copy the sentence.

We will go on a trip.

Part 6
Read the words and sentences.

yes	yell	sent	bet	letter	☐
last	slid	flip	flaps	fork	☐
morning	short	best	when	rush	☐
funny	fill	feel	cold	greets	☐

1. See me sleep in the green grass. ☐

2. The math class did not go well. ☐

(Parent's/Listener's) signature _____ Date _____

Directions, Part 5:
1. Read the directions to the student: *Copy the sentence.*
2. Tell the student: *Copy the sentence just as it is written. Remember to start with a capital letter and to put a period at the end of the sentence.*
Directions, Part 6:
1. Tell the student to read each row of words and the sentences.
2. Make a check mark in the box if the student reads all the words in the row or in the sentence correctly.

Name _____

Part 1
Draw the lines. Then write in the missing letters.

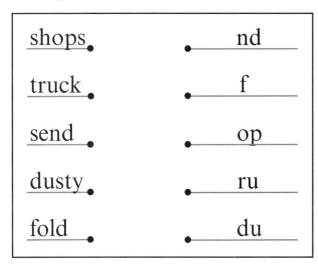

shops.	nd
truck.	f
send.	op
dusty.	ru
fold.	du

Part 2
Follow the lines and copy each sound.

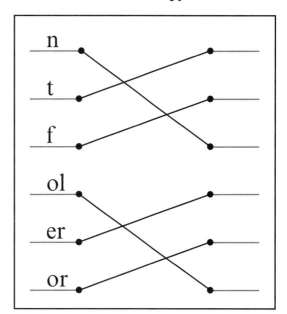

n

t

f

ol

er

or

Part 3
Circle the words.

(than) t h e n w h e n t h a t t h t a c k t h e n t h a n t h i s t h e t h e t h a n
t h a t h t h a n t h e n w h e n t h e t h i n g t h a n t h i s t h e t a c k

④

Part 4
Follow the lines and copy each word.

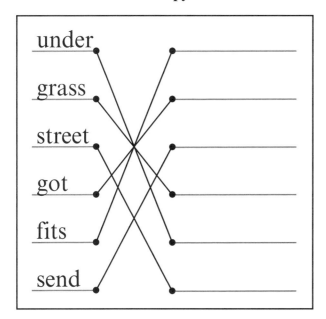

under

grass

street

got

fits

send

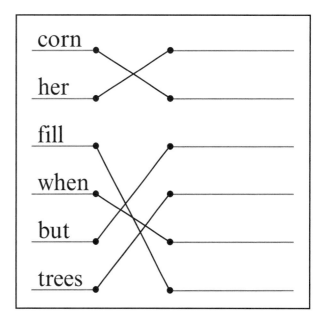

corn

her

fill

when

but

trees

Word completion, sound/symbol relationships, word matching, copying words

Part 5

Copy the sentences.

He will run up the hill.

_____

Her class went to the track meet.

_____

The men will sleep in that tent.

_____

Part 6

Read the words and sentences.

to	is	was	went	wish	→	☐
cuts	drip	short	felt	fold	→	☐
yes	hands	smell	steep	drop	→	☐
black	best	class	dust	green	→	☐

1. How can he sleep when we sing? ☐

2. That colt trots faster and faster. ☐

3. When they met, they felt happy. ☐

(Parent's/Listener's) signature _____ Date _____

Directions, Part 5:
1. Read the directions to the student: *Copy the sentences.*
2. Tell the student: *Copy each sentence just as it is written. Remember to start with a capital letter and to put a period at the end of each sentence.*

Directions, Part 6:
1. Tell the student to read each row of words and the sentences.
2. Make a check mark in the box if the student reads all the words in the row or in the sentence correctly.

Part 1

Follow the lines and copy each sound.

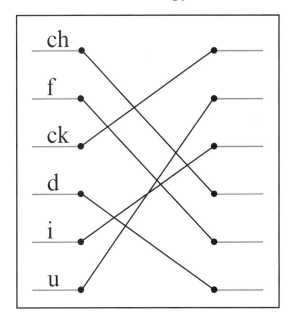

ch

f

ck

d

i

u

Part 2

Draw the lines. Then write in the missing letters.

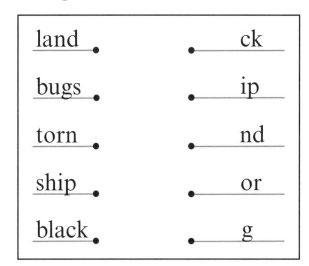

land ·   · ck

bugs ·   · ip

torn ·   · nd

ship ·   · or

black ·   · g

Part 3

Draw lines to match the words and pictures.

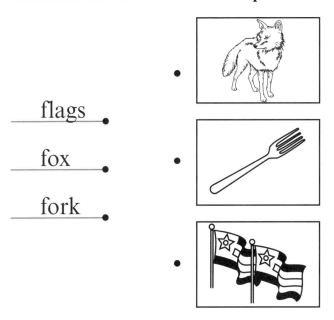

flags

fox

fork

Part 4

Follow the lines and copy each word.

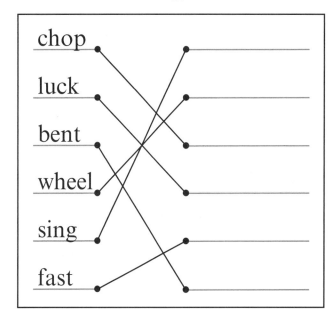

chop

luck

bent

wheel

sing

fast

Sound/symbol relationships, word completion, word recognition, copying words

Part 5

Follow the lines and copy each word.

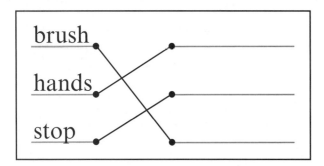
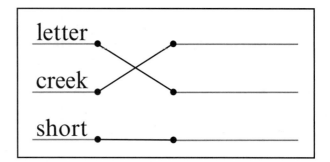

Part 6

Copy the sentences.

I will sleep in the green grass.

_____

She went to her swimming class.

_____

Part 7

Read the words and sentences.

crust	sunny	yet	they	yelling	☐
was	mats	black	gold	much	☐
chip	dropping	six	steps	camp	☐

☐

1. When will they stop sending me letters?

☐

2. The green bug was in that tree.

☐

3. They will lock the shed in the morning.

(Parent's/Listener's) signature _____ Date _____

Directions, Part 7:
1. Tell the student to read each row of words and the sentences.
2. Make a check mark in the box if the student reads all the words in the row or in the sentence correctly.

Name _____

Part 1

Draw the lines. Then write in the missing letters.

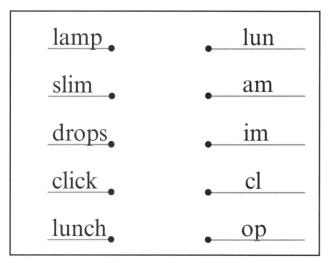

lamp	lun
slim	am
drops	im
click	cl
lunch	op

Part 2

Follow the lines and copy each sound.

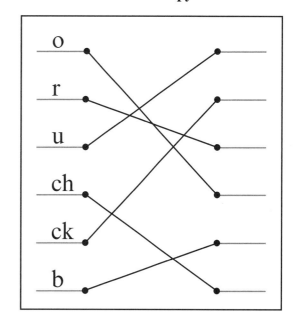

o
r
u
ch
ck
b

Part 3

Circle the sentence that tells about the picture.

The old cat sat on the bed.

The old cat hid under the bed.

The old cat sat in the tree.

Word completion, sound/symbol relationships, sentence reading

Part 4

Follow the lines and copy each word.

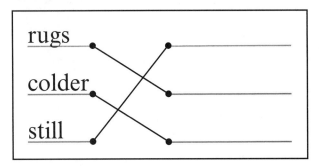
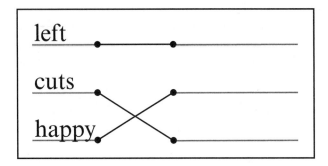

Part 5

Copy the sentences.

She sat in her truck.

_____

I am happy in this class.

_____

Part 6

Read the words and sentences.

told	to	was	yet	smell	☐
short	shore	store	plant	clip	☐
pan	faster	lend	next	fix	☐

1. They set up a tent at the creek. ☐

2. The pig got in the mud. ☐

3. He sent me a short letter. ☐

(Parent's/Listener's) signature _____ Date _____

Directions, Part 6:
1. Tell the student to read each row of words and the sentences.
2. Make a check mark in the box if the student reads all the words in the row or in the sentence correctly.

Part 1

Follow the lines and copy each sound.

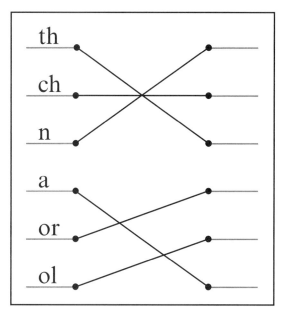

th

ch

n

a

or

ol

Part 2

Draw the lines. Then write in the missing letters.

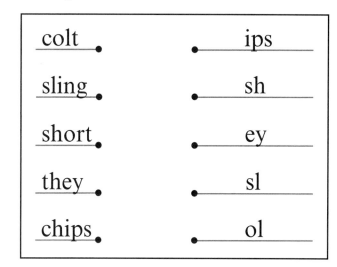

colt   ips

sling   sh

short   ey

they   sl

chips   ol

Part 3

Circle the words.

(left) l e t l e t t e r l i c k l e f t f i l l f l s l e d l e f t r e e f b e t t l e f t
l e g r e d l e f t b e t t e r l e n d l e f t e n d t e l l g e t l e f t l i p l i ⑥

Part 4

Follow the lines and copy each word.

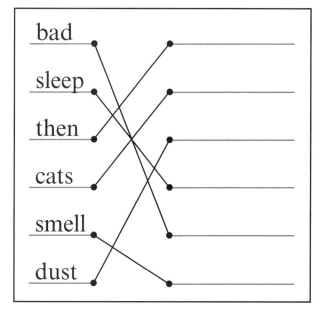

bad

sleep

then

cats

smell

dust

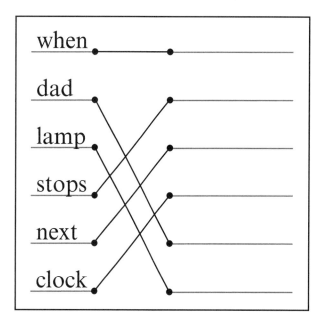

when

dad

lamp

stops

next

clock

Sound/symbol relationships, word completion, word matching, copying words

Part 5
Copy the sentences.

I will go to the store now.

_____

A black cat sat in that tree.

_____

She told me how happy she was.

_____

Part 6
Read the words and sentences.

bent	dents	dusty	creek	muddy	☐
sore	shore	shops	chop	bath	☐
slams	champ	clamp	block	picking	☐
yelling	still	fold	form	pens	☐

☐
☐
☐

1. Next week, we will go on a trip.

2. They had fish and chips for lunch.

3. Did he lock the shed yet?

(Parent's/Listener's) signature _____ Date _____

Directions, Part 6:
1. Tell the student to read each row of words and the sentences.
2. Make a check mark in the box if the student reads all the words in the row or in the sentence correctly.

Part 1

Draw the lines. Then write in the missing letters.

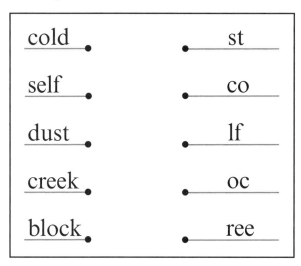

cold .	. st
self .	. co
dust .	. lf
creek .	. oc
block .	. ree

Part 2

Follow the lines and copy each sound.

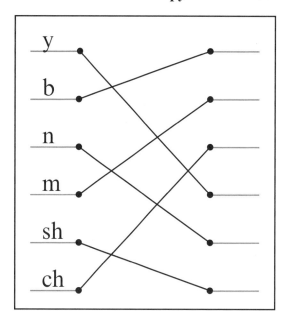

y

b

n

m

sh

ch

Part 3

Draw lines to match the words and pictures.

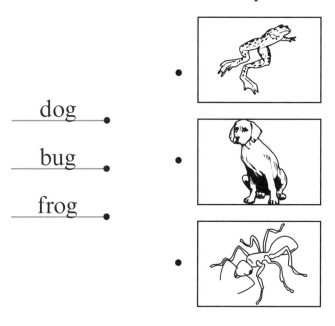

dog

bug

frog

Part 4

Follow the lines and copy each word.

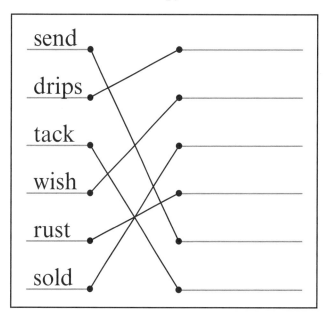

send

drips

tack

wish

rust

sold

Word completion, sound/symbol relationships, word recognition, copying words

Part 5

Follow the lines and copy each word.

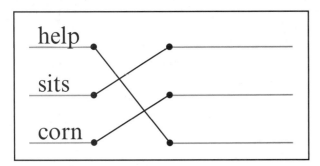
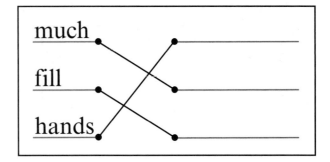

Part 6

Copy the sentence.

We went and sat under the tree.

_____

Part 7

Read the words and sentences.

glad	champ	much	such	stump		☐
do	to	dog	frog	form	said	☐
letters	north	better	left	list		☐

☐

1. If we rent a truck, we can go on a trip. ☐

2. She will help him lift that big box. ☐

3. His dog was muddy and wet.

(Parent's/Listener's) signature _____ Date _____

Directions, Part 7:
1. Tell the student to read each row of words and the sentences.
2. Make a check mark in the box if the student reads all the words in the row or in the sentence correctly.

Name _____

Part 1
Follow the lines and copy each sound.

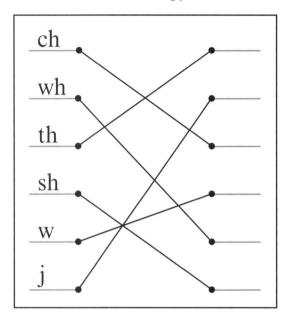

ch

wh

th

sh

w

j

Part 2
Draw the lines. Then write in the missing letters.

flips	en
steep	ow
then	top
town	lip
stops	eep

Part 3
Circle the sentence that tells about the picture.

This dog sat in the bathtub.

This dog sat in the box.

This frog sat in the box.

Sound/symbol relationships, word completion, sentence reading

Part 4

Follow the lines and copy each word.

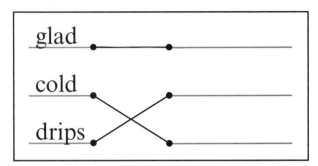

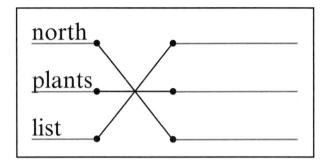

Part 5

Copy the sentences.

I can not fix this truck.

_____

Six men went to the camp.

_____

Part 6

Read the words and sentences.

jump	jam	plants	stand	still	☐
feel	fell	shelf	down	drops	☐
singer	mister	slips	such	next	☐

☐

1. She was the best runner in this town. ☐

2. He said, "Did the cat sleep under the bed?" ☐

3. The tracks led to a shack next to the hill. ☐

(Parent's/Listener's) signature _____ Date _____

Directions, Part 6:
1. Tell the student to read each row of words and the sentences.
2. Make a check mark in the box if the student reads all the words in the row or in the sentence correctly.

Part 1

Draw the lines. Then write in the missing letters.

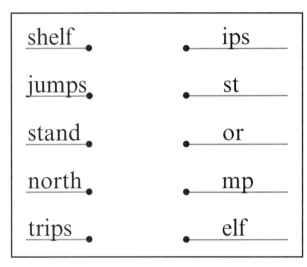

shelf	ips
jumps	st
stand	or
north	mp
trips	elf

Part 2

Follow the lines and copy each sound.

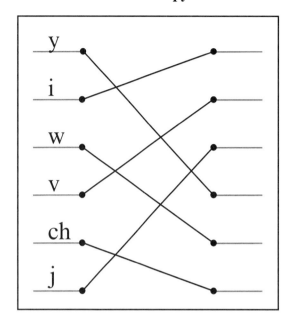

y
i
w
v
ch
j

Part 3

Draw lines to match the words and pictures.

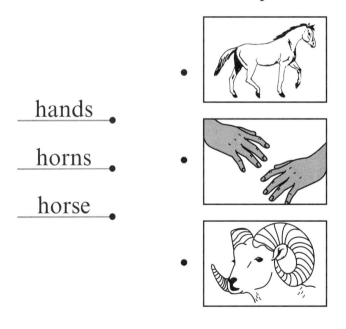

hands

horns

horse

Part 4

Follow the lines and copy each word.

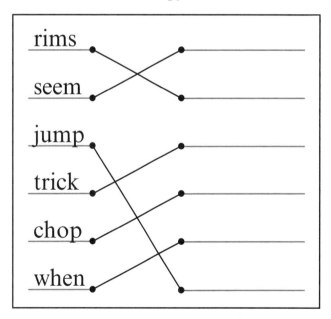

rims
seem
jump
trick
chop
when

Word completion, sound/symbol relationships, word recognition, copying words

Name _____

Part 5
Copy the sentences.

We ran up the steep hill.

_____

She will get jam at the store.

_____

Part 6
Follow the lines and copy each word.

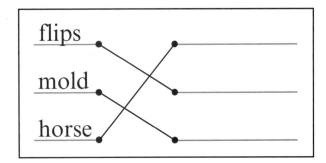

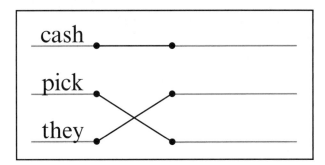

Part 7
Read the words and sentences.

grab	grin	singer	sending	smell	☐
clamp	champ	chops	tops	stop	☐
job	born	rust	desk	last	☐

1. That plant will fit on this shelf. ☐

2. His dusty dog needs a bath. ☐

3. She ate ham and corn for dinner. ☐

(Parent's/Listener's) signature _____ Date _____

Directions, Part 7:
1. Tell the student to read each row of words and the sentences.
2. Make a check mark in the box if the student reads all the words in the row or in the sentence correctly.

Name _____

Part 1
Follow the lines and copy each sound.

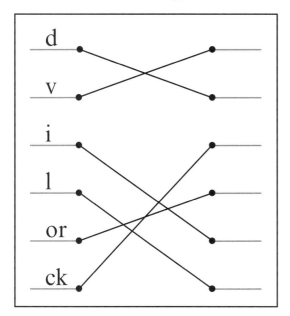

d

v

i

l

or

ck

Part 2
Draw the lines. Then write in the missing letters.

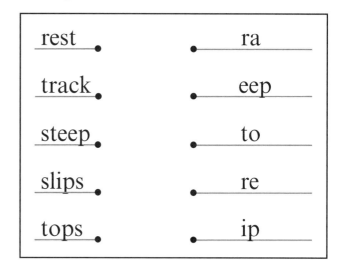

rest	ra
track	eep
steep	to
slips	re
tops	ip

Part 3
Circle the sentence that tells about the picture.

The bus went up the street.

The truck went up the street.

The bus went down the street.

Part 4
Circle the words.

(bad) b e s t b i d d a d b a d b o l t b o r n b i t s b a d s a d l a n d b a d l a
f a d d a s h b a d f a s t m a d p a l b a d s a n d f a s t b a d b o l d b e t

⑥

Sound/symbol relationships, word completion, sentence reading, word matching

Part 5

Copy the sentences.

The dog sat in the bathtub.

_____

He got a job at that store.

_____

Part 6

Follow the lines and copy each word.

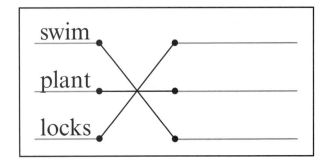

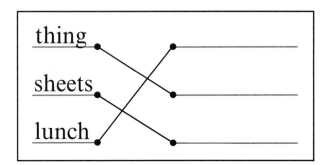

Part 7

Read the words and sentences.

| to | do | desk | rest | rush | hub | ☐ |

| what | when | then | town | swimming | ☐ |

| sunny | sleeps | grabs | yes | you | ☐ |

1. His dad said, "Go to the store now." ☐

2. Six green bugs hid under the rug. ☐

3. I can not smell this plant. ☐

(Parent's/Listener's) signature _____ Date _____

Directions, Part 7:
1. Tell the student to read each row of words and the sentences.
2. Make a check mark in the box if the student reads all the words in the row or in the sentence correctly.

Name _____

Part 1

Draw the lines. Then write in the missing letters.

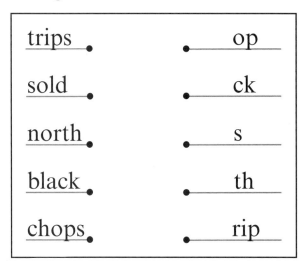

trips	op
sold	ck
north	s
black	th
chops	rip

Part 2

Follow the lines and copy each sound.

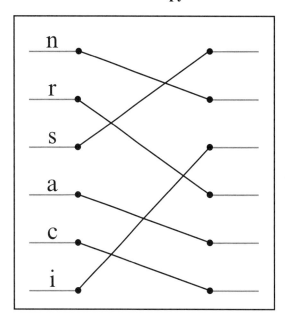

n

r

s

a

c

i

Part 3

Draw lines to match the words and pictures.

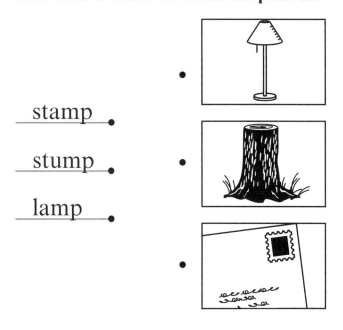

stamp

stump

lamp

Part 4

Follow the lines and copy each word.

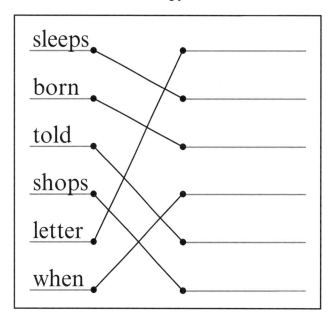

sleeps

born

told

shops

letter

when

Word completion, sound/symbol relationships, word recognition, copying words

Part 5
Copy the sentences.

We met at the swimming meet.

_____

They will stop for lunch now.

_____

Part 6
Follow the lines and copy each word.

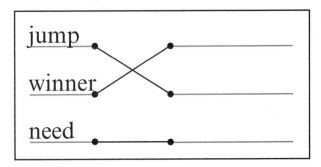

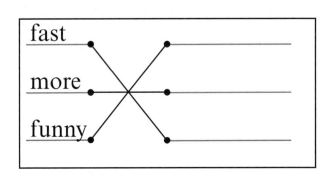

Part 7
Read the words and sentences.

of	what	was	shelf	vest	very	☐
jelly	just	tops	you	yelling		☐
to	thing	think	blink	swimmer		☐

1. She will sell her old truck. ☐

2. His dog sleeps on that red rug. ☐

3. He said, "Hand me the jam." ☐

(Parent's/Listener's) signature _____ Date _____

Directions, Part 7:
1. Tell the student to read each row of words and the sentences.
2. Make a check mark in the box if the student reads all the words in the row or in the sentence correctly.

Part 1
Follow the lines and copy each sound.

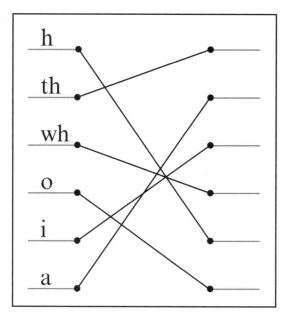

h

th

wh

o

i

a

Part 2
Draw the lines. Then write in the missing letters.

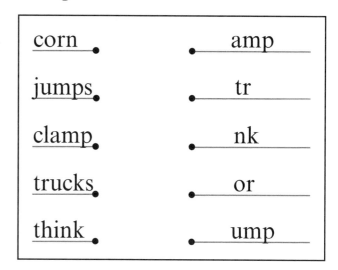

corn   amp

jumps   tr

clamp   nk

trucks   or

think   ump

Part 3
Circle the sentence that tells about the picture.

He has pants that fit.

He has socks that fit.

He has pants that do not fit.

Part 4
Circle the words.

(pin) p a n l i p p i n s h i p p e n i p p i t p i n p i g p a n p e t p i n

t r i p f i t p a n p i n l i p p e n s p i n p a t p e t p i n p i g c l i p

⑥

Sound/symbol relationships, word completion, sentence reading, word matching

Part 5

Follow the lines and copy each word.

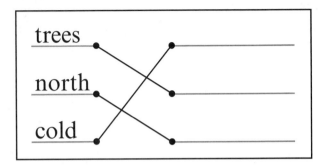

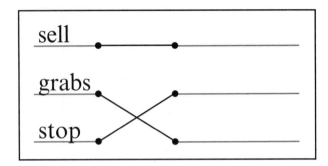

Part 6

Copy the sentences.

He told me how to get to the store.

_____

Her dog sleeps on that old rug.

_____

Part 7

Read the words and sentences.

check	think	things	told	planting
morning	grips	lunch	stuck	steep
felt	very	jumping	was	wishing

1. She said, "When do you go to class?"

2. They sat down on an ant hill.

3. We will send a gift to her.

(Parent's/Listener's) signature _____ Date _____

Directions, Part 7:
1. Tell the student to read each row of words and the sentences.
2. Make a check mark in the box if the student reads all the words in the row or in the sentence correctly.

Name _____

Part 1

Draw the lines. Then write in the missing letters.

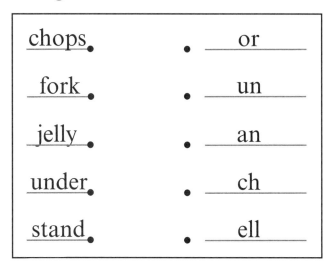

chops •   • ___ or ___

fork •   • ___ un ___

jelly •   • ___ an ___

under •   • ___ ch ___

stand •   • ___ ell ___

Part 2

Follow the lines and copy each sound.

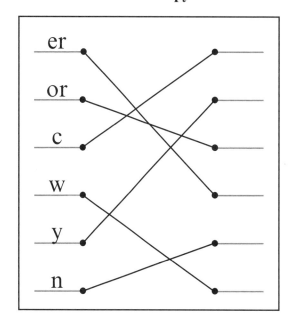

er

or

c

w

y

n

Part 3

Circle the sentence that tells about the picture.

The frog sat next to the old truck.

The frog sat on top of the old truck.

The frog sat under the old truck.

Part 4

Circle the words.

(belt) b e t b e l l b e l t l e f t w e l l f e l t b e l t l e t l e n d f e l t b e l t l ⑤
b e t s f e l l t e l l b e l t f e l t s e l l l e f t s e n d b e l t l e f t e n d f e

Word completion, sound/symbol relationships, sentence reading, word matching

Name _____

Part 5

Follow the lines and copy each word.

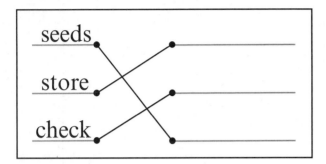

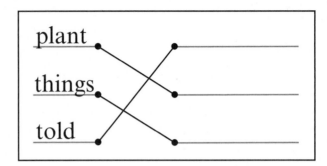

Part 6

Copy the sentences.

They had lots of desks in the class.

_____

The horse ran on a dusty path.

_____

Part 7

Read the words and sentences.

butter	under	damp	after	mast	☐
than	hold	when	clocks	you	☐
stops	shop	what	lots	list	☐

1. She was the best singer in town. ☐

2. They sat on a hill next to the pond. ☐

3. He said, "I feel much better now." ☐

(Parent's/Listener's) signature _____ Date _____

Directions, Part 7:
1. Tell the student to read each row of words and the sentences.
2. Make a check mark in the box if the student reads all the words in the row or in the sentence correctly.

Name _____

Part 1

Follow the lines and copy each sound.

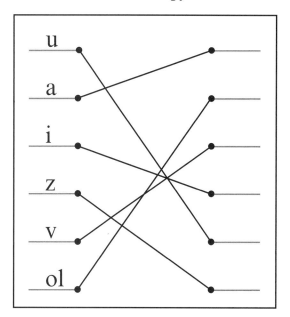

u
a
i
z
v
ol

Part 2

Draw the lines. Then write in the missing letters.

smell	•	•	ch
after	•	•	ell
hold	•	•	ow
check	•	•	er
town	•	•	ol

Part 3

Circle the sentence that tells about the picture.

This clock will not run.

This clock will run very well.

This clock did not stop.

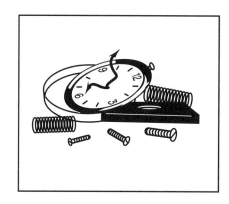

Part 4

Circle the words.

(wish) dishwishcashmifishlistwishwillwinwishw
inwillfishwishmashmistlastwillwishwith

⑤

Sound/symbol relationships, word completion, sentence reading, word matching

Part 5

Follow the lines and copy each word.

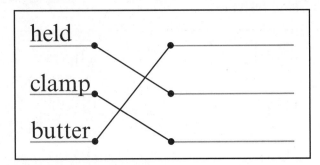

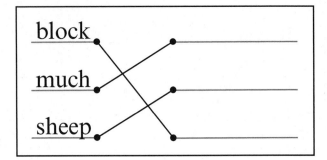

Part 6

Copy the sentences.

You left lots of things on her desk.

_____

Six men will camp on that hill.

_____

Part 7

Read the words and sentences.

things	winner	chopping	what	after	☐
slip	stuck	silly	clapping	spring	☐
store	cold	lucky	very	shelf	☐

1. Can we swim in that pond?   ☐

2. Bud said, "I will fix a big dinner."   ☐

3. Her left leg is in a cast.   ☐

(Parent's/Listener's) signature _____ Date _____

Directions, Part 7:
1. Tell the student to read each row of words and the sentences.
2. Make a check mark in the box if the student reads all the words in the row or in the sentence correctly.

Name _____

Part 1

Draw the lines. Then write in the missing letters.

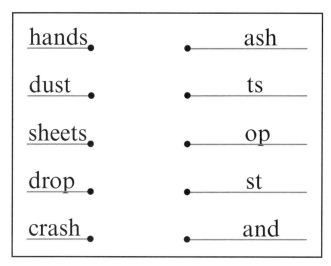

hands	ash
dust	ts
sheets	op
drop	st
crash	and

Part 2

Follow the lines and copy each sound.

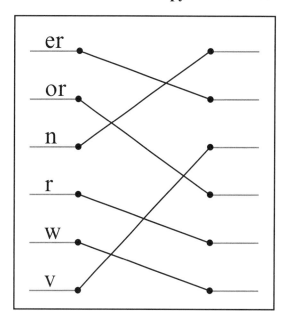

er
or
n
r
w
v

Part 3

Draw lines to match the words and pictures.

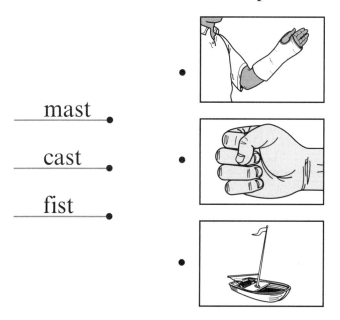

mast
cast
fist

Part 4

Follow the lines and copy each word.

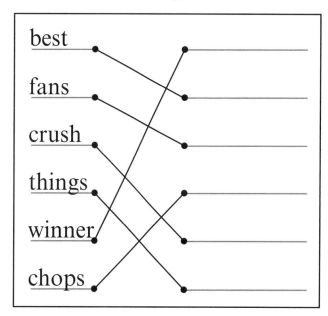

best
fans
crush
things
winner
chops

Word completion, sound/symbol relationships, word recognition, copying words

Part 5

Copy the sentences.

An old truck went down the street.

_____

His black cat sat in his lap.

_____

Part 6

Follow the lines and copy each word.

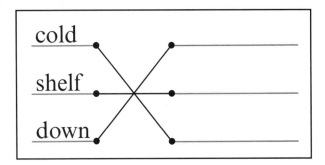

cold _____

shelf _____

down _____

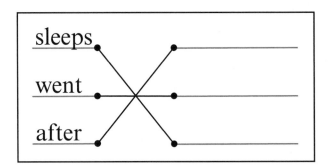

sleeps _____

went _____

after _____

Part 7

Read the words and sentences.

think	spring	of	slick	you	☐
planting	things	next	letters	do	☐
stops	stamp	which	hammer	grip	☐

1. Help her fix that clock now. ☐

2. His mom said, "What did you do this morning?" ☐

3. When did they get on the bus? ☐

(Parent's/Listener's) signature _____ Date _____

Directions, Part 7:
1. Tell the student to read each row of words and the sentences.
2. Make a check mark in the box if the student reads all the words in the row or in the sentence correctly.

Part 1
Follow the lines and copy each sound.

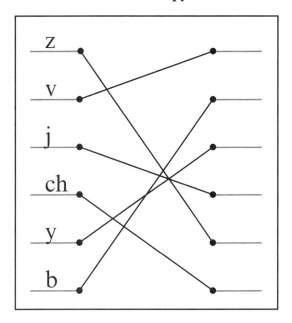

z ____

v ____

j ____

ch ____

y ____

b ____

Part 2
Draw the lines. Then write in the missing letters.

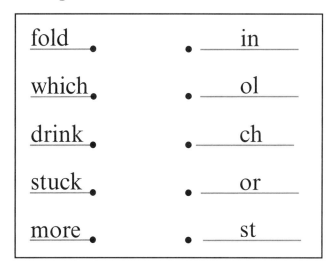

fold •   • ____ in ____

which •   • ____ ol ____

drink •   • ____ ch ____

stuck •   • ____ or ____

more •   • ____ st ____

Part 3
Draw lines to match the words and pictures.

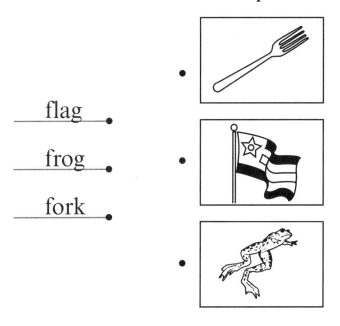

flag ____ •

frog ____ •

fork ____ •

Part 4
Follow the lines and copy each word.

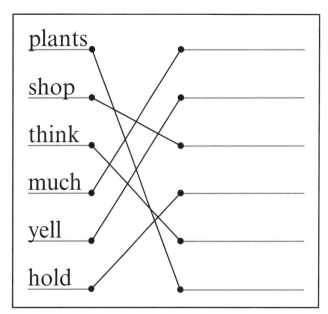

plants ____

shop ____

think ____

much ____

yell ____

hold ____

Sound/symbol relationships, word completion, word recognition, copying words

Name _____

Part 5
Copy the sentences.

The wet street is slick.

_____

Her mom lost her green hat.

_____

Part 6
Follow the lines and copy each word.

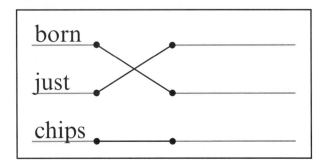
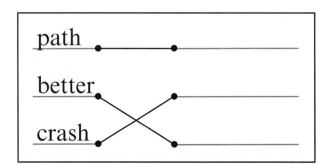

Part 7
Read the words and sentences.

funny	needs	lost	stops	store	→	☐
stamps	stink	quick	which	shelf	→	☐
rent	swinging	what	of	happy	→	☐

1. Do not step on that rug with muddy feet.   ☐

2. When will we get to the next town?   ☐

3. She said, "I did not see you in math class."   ☐

(Parent's/Listener's) signature _____ Date _____

Directions, Part 7:
1. Tell the student to read each row of words and the sentences.
2. Make a check mark in the box if the student reads all the words in the row or in the sentence correctly.

Name _____

Part 1
Draw the lines. Then write in the missing letters.

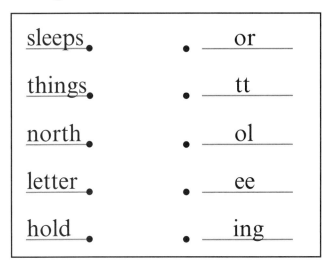

sleeps	or
things	tt
north	ol
letter	ee
hold	ing

Part 2
Follow the lines and copy each sound.

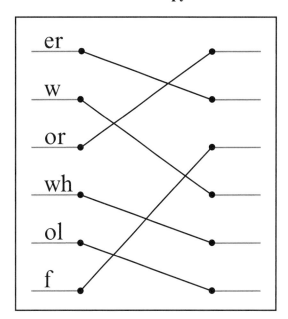

er
w
or
wh
ol
f

Part 3
Draw lines to match the words and pictures.

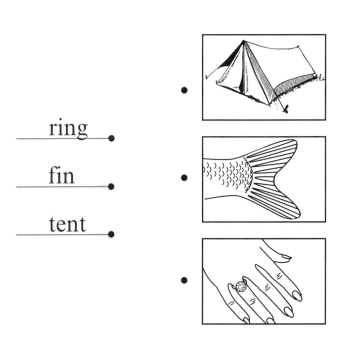

ring

fin

tent

Part 4
Follow the lines and copy each word.

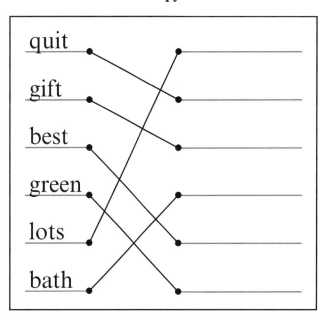

quit
gift
best
green
lots
bath

Word completion, sound/symbol relationships, word recognition, copying words

Part 5

Copy the sentences.

A skunk sat on that old stump.

_____

They will fix dinner now.

_____

Part 6

Follow the lines and copy each word.

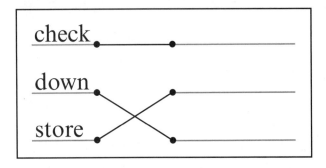

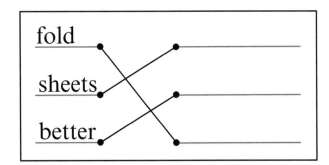

Part 7

Read the words and sentences.

lamp	then	grins	think	which	☐
of	what	stops	black	now	☐
sitting	lucky	fits	jumps	lost	☐

☐
☐
☐

1. We got this clock at a junk shop.

2. "Do not fill that tub to the top," he said.

3. You will do well in the next class.

(Parent's/Listener's) signature _____ Date _____

Directions, Part 7:
1. Tell the student to read each row of words and the sentences.
2. Make a check mark in the box if the student reads all the words in the row or in the sentence correctly.

Answer Key

Name _____

Part 1
Draw lines to match the sounds.

r
a
f
t
e
th

t
f
a
th
e
r

Part 2
Write in the missing letters.

sit — ma**s**t
ham — si**t**
mast — ha**m**

Part 3
Draw lines to match the words and pictures.

feet
cat

Sound/symbol relationships, word completion, word recognition

Lesson 11　　1

Name _____

Part 4
Circle the sounds.

t h r h d (th) i m d h e r h (th) a s m d e   ④
m (th) s m h t e r d a (th) m h t i r s

c i a m d (c) t e s d a i t (c) a f r i t m   ④
d a t i e f i d (c) a i m t s i a (c) d t

f i r d a (f) o d i e d r (f) t h m r s (f)   ⑦
r d c i f (f) a c d i r s f d i c (f) t h a

Part 5
Follow the lines and copy each word.

that → *hat*
this → *the*
feed → *that*
hat → *this*
the → *feed*

Sound/symbol relationships, copying words

2　　*Lesson 11*

113

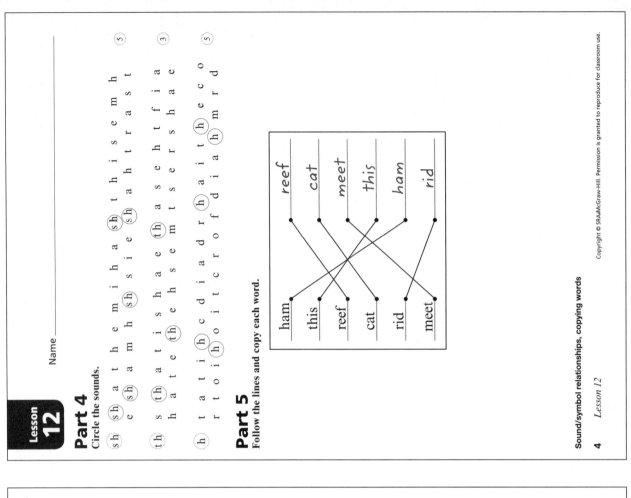

Lesson 12

Name _____

Part 1
Draw lines to match the sounds.

m
a
s
e
t
r

a
t
e
s
r
m

Part 2
Write in the missing letters.

reef
ram
hid
hat

hid
hat
reef
ram

Part 3
Draw lines to match the words and pictures.

ram
hat
rat

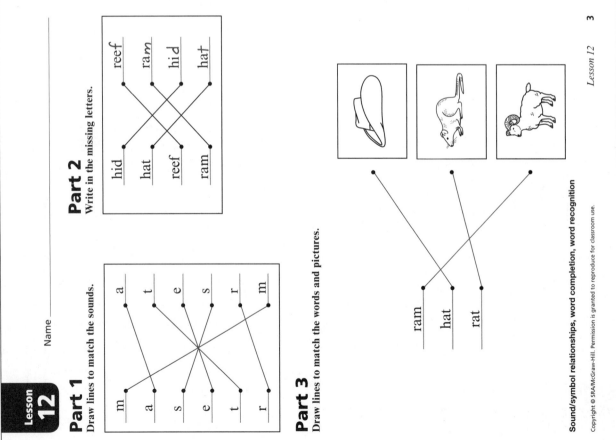

Sound/symbol relationships, word completion, word recognition

Lesson 12   3

Copyright © SRA/McGraw-Hill. Permission is granted to reproduce for classroom use.

Lesson 12

Name _____

Part 4
Circle the sounds.

sh (sh) a t h e m i h a (sh) t h i s e m h
e (sh) a m h (sh) s i e (sh) a h t r a s t   (5)

th (th) a t i s h a e (th) a s e h t f i a
h a t e (th) e h s e m t s e r s h a e   (3)

h t a t i (h) c d i a d r (h) a i t (h) e c o
r t o i (h) o i t c r o f f d i a (h) m r d   (5)

Part 5
Follow the lines and copy each word.

reef
cat
meet
this
ham
rid

ham
this
reef
cat
rid
meet

Sound/symbol relationships, copying words

4   *Lesson 12*

Copyright © SRA/McGraw-Hill. Permission is granted to reproduce for classroom use.

114

Name _____

Part 1
Draw lines to match the sounds.

i — sh
f — th
h — c
c — h
th — f
sh — i

Part 2
Write in the missing letters.

feed — cam
cam — this
this — hat
hat — feed

Part 3
Draw lines to match the words and pictures.

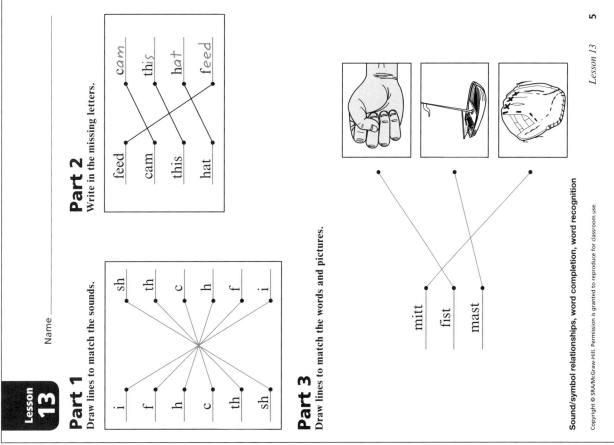

mitt
fist
mast

Name _____

Part 4
Circle the sounds.

f t h i t (f) i m i d (f) c t r i a e i (f) ⑦
e (f) m i m i (f) c e (f) d i h t a m

(th) t s h i p a (th) a e h a s e h t f p i ④
h i (th) a h e h s a e m (th) e a r s t m

sh h e t (sh) e d i e d (sh) e i t h i t c r ⑤
r t o c r i (sh) e r s i e h c (sh) d d i

Part 5
Follow the lines and copy each word.

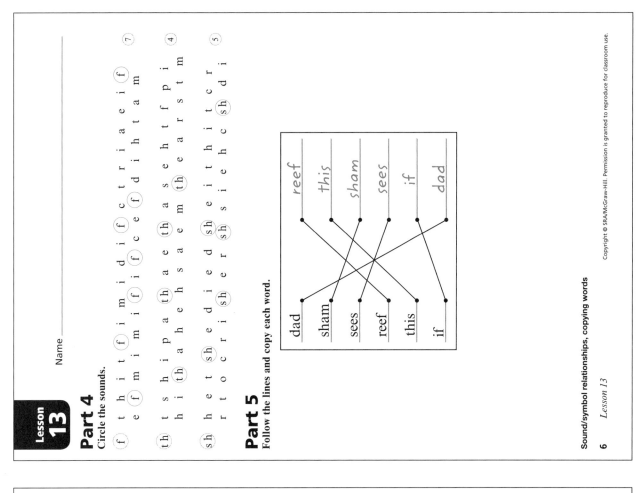

dad — reef
sham — this
sees — sham
reef — sees
this — if
if — dad

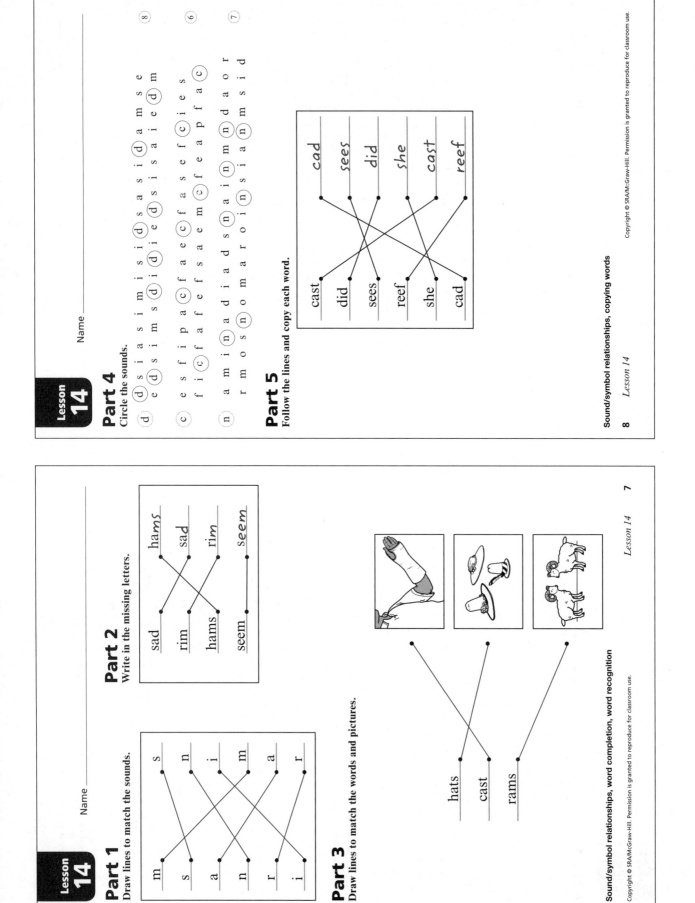

Lesson 14

Name _____

Part 1
Draw lines to match the sounds.

m   s
s   n
a   i
n   m
r   a
i   r

Part 2
Write in the missing letters.

sad — hams
rim — sad
hams — rim
seem — seem

Part 3
Draw lines to match the words and pictures.

hats
cast
rams

Sound/symbol relationships, word completion, word recognition

Lesson 14   7

Lesson 14

Name _____

Part 4
Circle the sounds.

d   d s i a s i m i s i d s a s i d a m s e
e d s i m s d i d i e d s i s a i e d m   ⑧

c   e s f i p a c f a e c f a s e f c i e s
f i c f a f f s a e m c f e a p f a c   ⑥

n   a m i n a d i a d s n a i n m n d a o r
r m o s n o m a r o i n s i a n m s i d   ⑦

Part 5
Follow the lines and copy each word.

cad
sees
did
she
cast
reef

cast
did
sees
reef
she
cad

8   *Lesson 14*

Part 4
Circle the sounds.

r m (r) e a (r) e m f (r) i m s a (r) e m a s   ⑦

e m (r) e m (r) m a m e i m i e (r) a i m   ⑤

(sh) c (sh) i p a t h a e (sh) a e c h p
h i (sh) a h e h s a e m t h e a i (sh)   ⑥

a (a) h i n a m e (a) m s n a i r h m e n r
r h e s n t h (a) r i n s i a n m h t s i

Part 5
Follow the lines and copy each word.

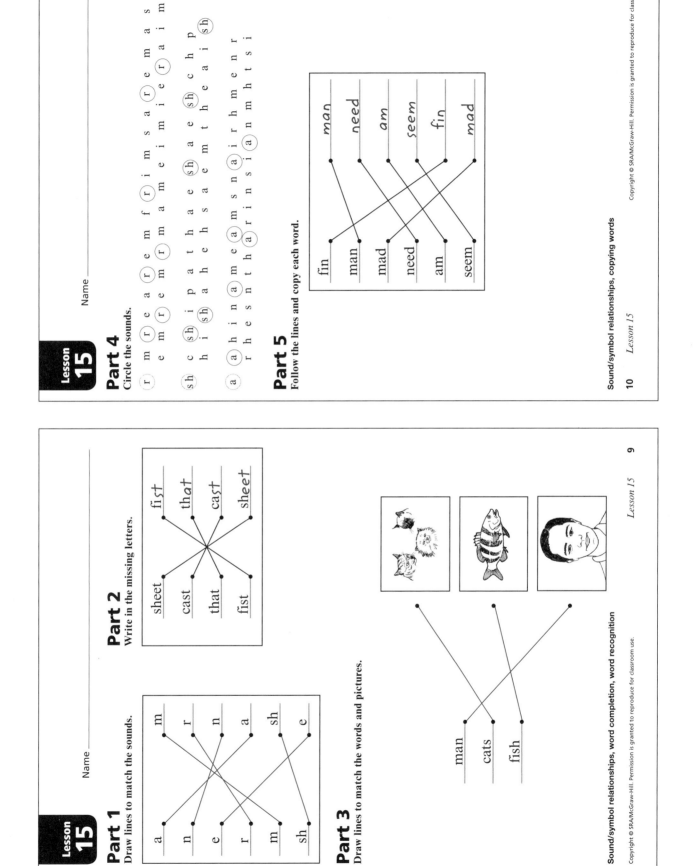

fin	man
man	need
mad	am
need	seem
am	fin
seem	mad

Part 1
Draw lines to match the sounds.

a — m
n — r
e — n
r — a
m — sh
sh — e

Part 2
Write in the missing letters.

sheet — fist
cast — that
that — cast
fist — sheet

Part 3
Draw lines to match the words and pictures.

man
cats
fish

117

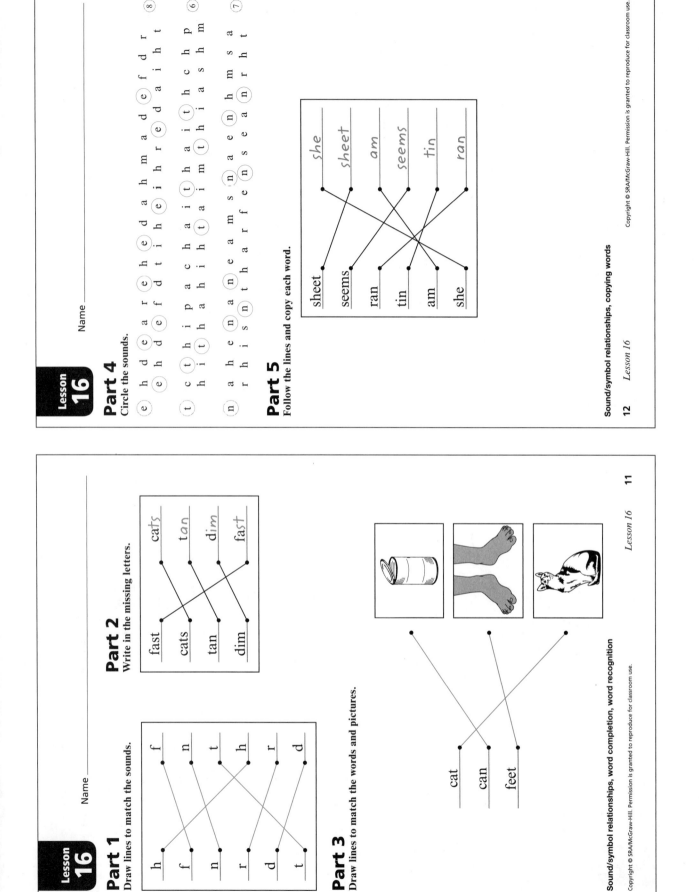

118

Lesson 16

Name _____

Part 1
Draw lines to match the sounds.

h
f
n
r
d
t

f
n
t
h
r
d

Part 2
Write in the missing letters.

fast — cats
cats — tan
tan — dim
dim — fast

Part 3
Draw lines to match the words and pictures.

cat
can
feet

Sound/symbol relationships, word completion, word recognition

Lesson 16   **11**

Copyright © SRA/McGraw-Hill. Permission is granted to reproduce for classroom use.

Lesson 16

Name _____

Part 4
Circle the sounds.

e h d e a r e h e d a h m a d e f d r   ⑧
e h d e f d t i h e i h r e d a i h t

t c t h i p a c h a i t h c h p   ⑥
h i t h a h h a i m t h i a s h m

n a h e n a n e a m s n a e n h m s a   ⑦
r h i s n t h a r f e n s e a n r h t

Part 5
Follow the lines and copy each word.

sheet .... she
seems .... sheet
ran .... am
tin .... seems
am .... tin
she .... ran

Sound/symbol relationships, copying words

12   *Lesson 16*

Copyright © SRA/McGraw-Hill. Permission is granted to reproduce for classroom use.

Lesson 17

Name _____

Part 1
Follow the lines and copy each sound.

m   r
e   c
r   m
d   e
th   d
c   th

Part 2
Write in the missing letters.

fish   him
had   fish
him   sat
sat   had

Part 3
Draw lines to match the words and pictures.

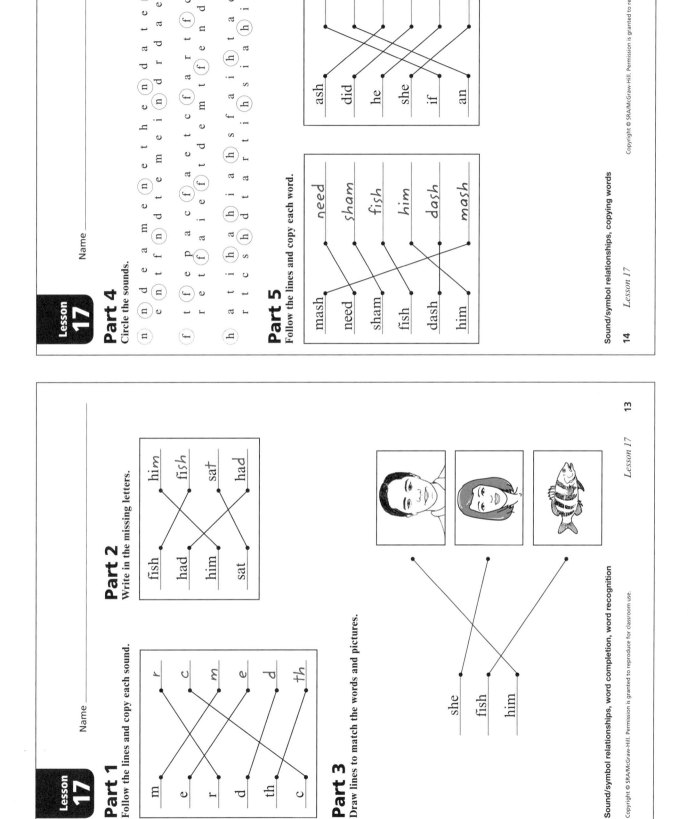

she
fish
him

Sound/symbol relationships, word completion, word recognition

Copyright © SRA/McGraw-Hill. Permission is granted to reproduce for classroom use.

Lesson 17   13

Lesson 17

Name _____

Part 4
Circle the sounds.

n d e a m e (n) e t h e (n) d a t e (n) d m   (7)
e (n) t f (n) d t e m e i (n) d r d a e a f i   (7)

f t f e p a e t c (f) a r t (f) c p e   (7)
r e t (f) a i e (f) t d e m t (f) e n d i t r   (7)

(h) a t i (h) i a (h) s f a i (h) t a c d t   (7)
r t c s (h) d t a r t i s i a (h) i s r a   (7)

Part 5
Follow the lines and copy each word.

mash   need
need   sham
sham   fish
fish   him
dash   dash
him   mash

if   ash
an   did
ash   he
did   she
he   if
she   an

Sound/symbol relationships, copying words

14   *Lesson 17*

Copyright © SRA/McGraw-Hill. Permission is granted to reproduce for classroom use.

119

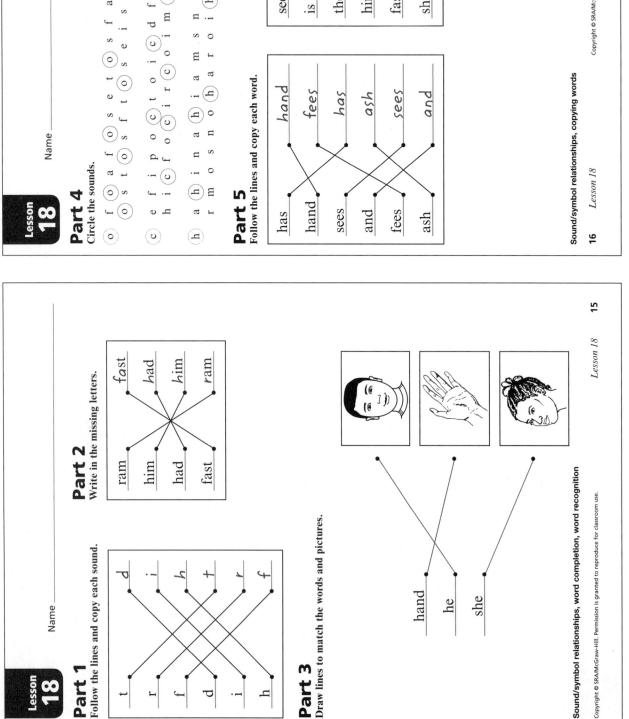

Lesson 18

Name _____

Part 1
Follow the lines and copy each sound.

t   d
r   i
f   h
d   t
i   r
h   f

Part 2
Write in the missing letters.

ram   fast
him   had
had   him
fast   ram

Part 3
Draw lines to match the words and pictures.

hand

he

she

Sound/symbol relationships, word completion, word recognition

Lesson 18   **15**

Lesson 18

Name _____

Part 4
Circle the sounds.

o   f o a f o s e t o s f a t o s h e f a s ⑧
o s t o s f t o s e i s f r f a o t e f r

c e f i p o c t o i c d f o i c f e f o d ⑧
h i c f o c i r c o i m c f i o a m c p e

h a h i n a h i a m s n e i n h a m o r ⑥
r m o s n o h a r o i h s i a n h i n n r

Part 5
Follow the lines and copy each word.

has   hand
hand   fees
sees   has
and   ash
fees   sees
ash   and

seeds   she
is   fast
the   him
him   the
fast   is
she   seeds

Sound/symbol relationships, copying words

Lesson 18   **16**

Name _____

Part 4
Circle the sounds.

ⓗ m e n t ⓗ m a n t ⓗ i n f d ⓗ o n f m e n ⑥
   h r n s m i n d ⓗ e m n f t m o n d ⓗ s n

ⓣⓗ m e ⓣⓗ d n e f m t f i ⓣⓗ s h i h ⓣⓗ f o ⑤
   e h ⓣⓗ e f t o h f n a m ⓣⓗ e n f m e d

ⓣ ⓣ h e l d m i a n d e i h f ⓣ n e d e f e r ⑥
   s m e n ⓣ h f d n e ⓣ m e ⓣⓗ d i a f ⓣ d f

Part 5
Follow the lines and copy each word.

hand	*rod*
mist	*has*
rod	*cot*
that	*that*
has	*mist*
cot	*hand*

cats	*hits*
had	*cats*
she	*had*
hits	*that*
am	*am*
that	*she*

Name _____

Part 1
Follow the lines and copy each sound.

o	*e*
th	*o*
e	*th*
sh	*f*
a	*sh*
f	*a*

Part 2
Write in the missing letters.

the	*has*
ash	*fins*
fins	*the*
has	*ash*

Part 3
Draw lines to match the words and pictures.

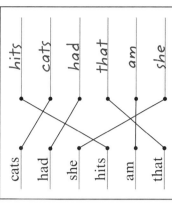
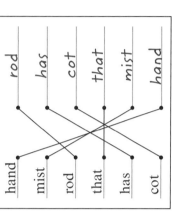

ram

cast

fist

121

Lesson 20

Part 1
Follow the lines and copy each sound.

sh — *th*
f — *n*
i — *r*
th — *sh*
r — *i*
n — *f*

Part 2
Write in the missing letters.

ant — *this*
this — *hot*
dash — *ant*
hot — *dash*

Part 3
Draw lines to match the words and pictures.

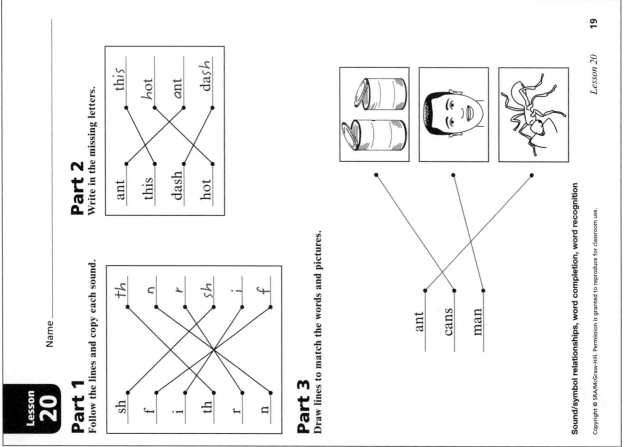

ant
cans
man

Sound/symbol relationships, word completion, word recognition

Lesson 20   19

Lesson 20

Name _____

Part 4
Follow the lines and copy each word.

sheet — *rid*
rid — *mash*
rod — *rod*
teeth — *sheet*
not — *not*
mash — *teeth*

math — *did*
dish — *math*
ant — *dish*
did — *and*
this — *ant*
and — *this*

Part 5
Read the words.

ram	sheets	fast	dim
cast	she	fish	him
seeds	feet	did	cat
am	cats	fins	that

☐ ☐ ☐ ☐

(Parent's/Listener's) signature _____ Date _____

Directions, Part 5:
1. Tell the student to read each row of words.
2. Make a check mark in the box if the student reads all the words in the row correctly.

20   *Lesson 20*

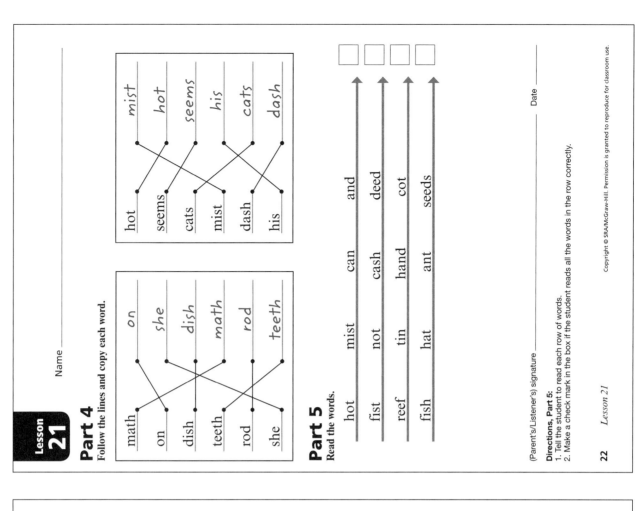

Lesson 21

Name _____

Part 4
Follow the lines and copy each word.

math — on
on — she
dish — dish
teeth — math
rod — rod
she — teeth

hot — mist
seems — hot
cats — seems
mist — his
dash — cats
his — dash

Part 5
Read the words.

hot	mist	can	and
fist	not	cash	deed
reef	tin	hand	cot
fish	hat	ant	seeds

☐ ☐ ☐ ☐

(Parent's/Listener's signature) _____ Date _____

Directions, Part 5:
1. Tell the student to read each row of words.
2. Make a check mark in the box if the student reads all the words in the row correctly.

22   *Lesson 21*   Copyright © SRA/McGraw-Hill. Permission is granted to reproduce for classroom use.

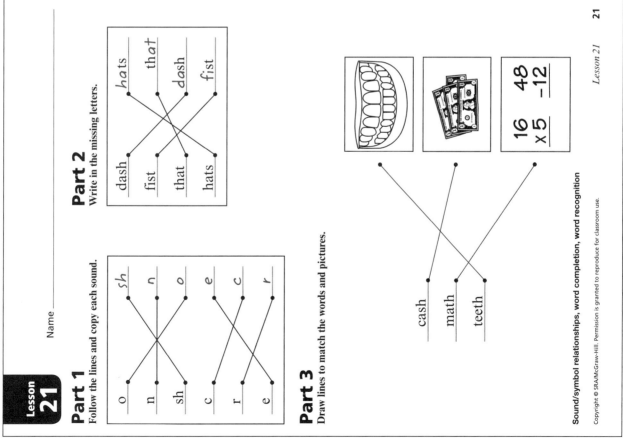

Lesson 21

Name _____

Part 1
Follow the lines and copy each sound.

o — sh
n — n
sh — o
c — e
r — c
e — r

Part 2
Write in the missing letters.

dash — hats
fist — that
that — dash
hats — fist

Part 3
Draw lines to match the words and pictures.

cash
math
teeth

Sound/symbol relationships, word completion, word recognition

Copyright © SRA/McGraw-Hill. Permission is granted to reproduce for classroom use.   *Lesson 21*   **21**

123

Part 1
Follow the lines and copy each sound.

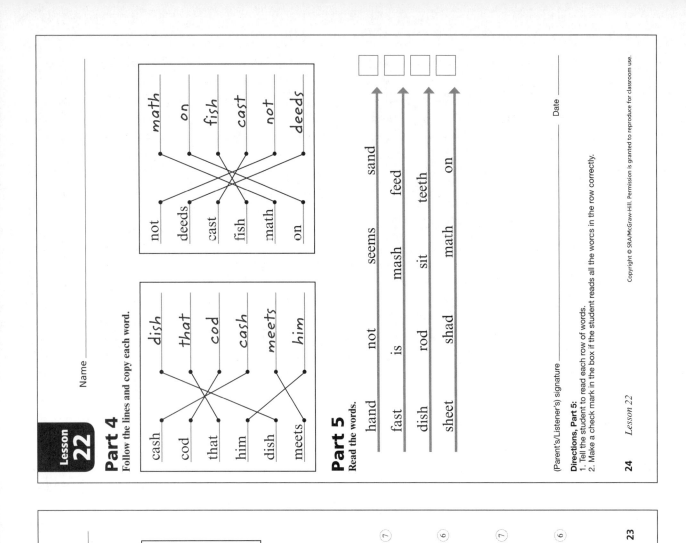

ing	*sh*
g	*m*
m	*th*
th	*n*
n	*ing*
sh	*g*

Part 2
Write in the missing letters.

rims	*than*
teeth	*cash*
than	*rims*
cash	*teeth*

Part 3
Circle the sounds.

g   t d f f e g r i a t r f d ⓖ e a o i m n t h   ⑦
    h a o i n t ⓖ h c s h m o f f r i ⓖ a h t h
    r e i m o n f ⓖ s e i h r ⓖ f t d m i o ⓖ

o   m s t d f c s h ⓞ a e r i h t h n m e r f   ⑥
    ⓖ o t c i m n r e ⓞ f s g h t i a c d o r
    a m n e ⓞ a r i s r d ⓞ g a r s i f t m t

f   d t r ⓕ e o g h i a ⓕ m n e o h g t r ⓕ e   ⑦
    i o n c m ⓕ r t i s a g n e a m r ⓕ t h g
    n m c a d e s a ⓕ t i o m n a d ⓕ t h e t

c   a e f g ⓒ o i m n g f d e s a t r ⓕ g ⓒ i   ⑥
    m n d f r e a s f ⓒ e d o i ⓒ a g r t s e
    n f g t ⓒ a t r i m n n o t ⓒ o t d i n a m

Sound/symbol relationships, word completion

Copyright © SRA/McGraw-Hill. Permission is granted to reproduce for classroom use.

Lesson 22   23

Part 4
Follow the lines and copy each word.

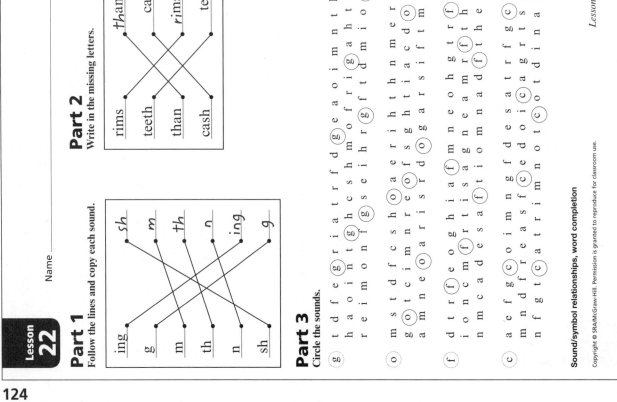

cash	*dish*
cod	*that*
that	*cod*
him	*cash*
dish	*meets*
meets	*him*

not	*math*
deeds	*on*
cast	*fish*
fish	*cast*
math	*not*
on	*deeds*

☐ ☐ ☐ ☐

Part 5
Read the words.

hand	not	seems	sand
fast	is	mash	feed
dish	rod	sit	teeth
sheet	shad	math	on

(Parent's/Listener's) signature _____   Date _____

Directions, Part 5:
1. Tell the student to read each row of words.
2. Make a check mark in the box if the student reads all the words in the row correctly.

24   *Lesson 22*

Copyright © SRA/McGraw-Hill. Permission is granted to reproduce for classroom use.

Name _____

Part 4
Follow the lines and copy each word.

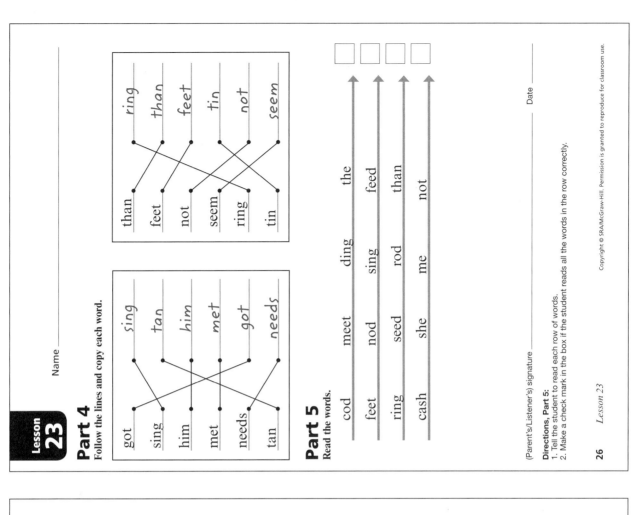

than	_ring_
feet	_than_
not	_feet_
seem	_tin_
ring	_not_
tin	_seem_

got	_sing_
sing	_tan_
him	_him_
met	_met_
needs	_got_
tan	_needs_

Part 5
Read the words.

☐ ☐ ☐ ☐

cod	meet	ding	the
feet	nod	sing	feed
ring	seed	rod	than
cash	she	me	not

(Parent's/Listener's signature) _____ Date _____

Directions, Part 5:
1. Tell the student to read each row of words.
2. Make a check mark in the box if the student reads all the words in the row correctly.

Name _____

Part 1
Follow the lines and copy each sound.

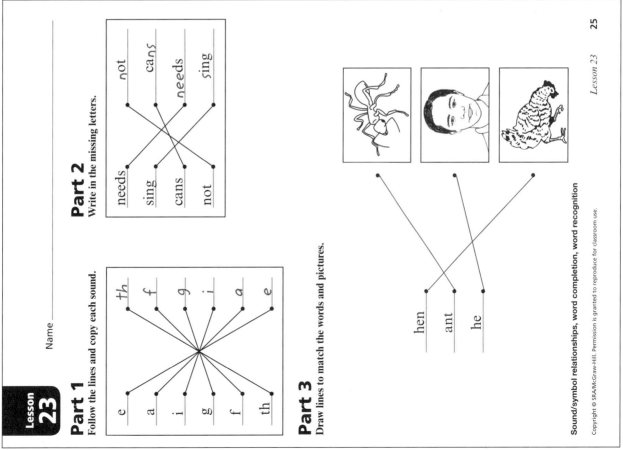

e	_th_
a	_f_
i	_g_
g	_i_
f	_a_
th	_e_

Part 2
Write in the missing letters.

needs	_not_
sing	_cans_
cans	_needs_
not	_sing_

Part 3
Draw lines to match the words and pictures.

hen

ant

he

Sound/symbol relationships, word completion, word recognition

125

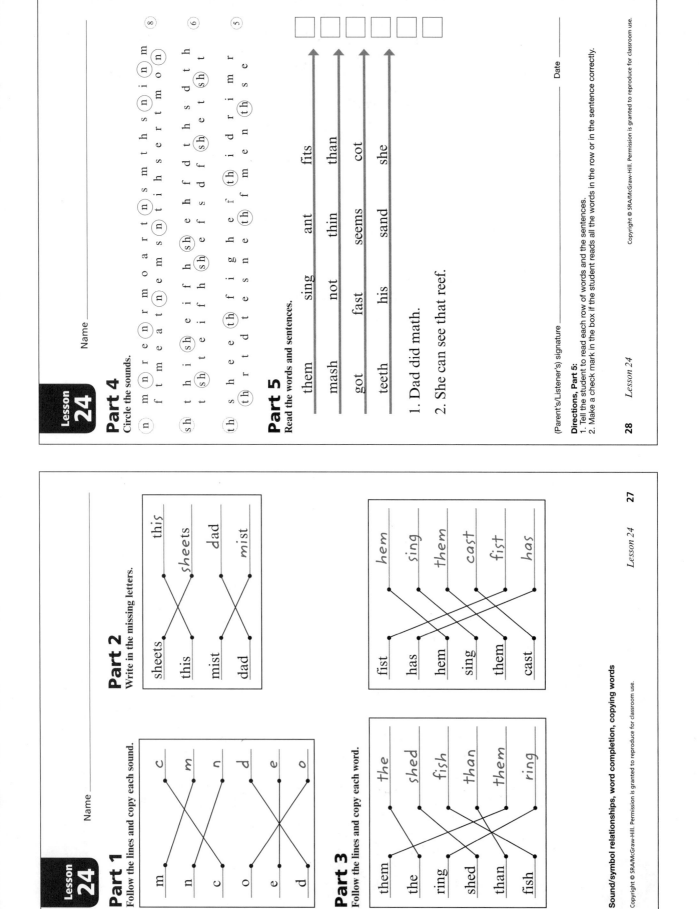

Lesson 24

126

Name _____

Part 1
Follow the lines and copy each sound.

m
n
c
o
e
d

c
m
n
d
e
o

Part 2
Write in the missing letters.

sheets — this
this — sheets
mist — dad
dad — mist

Part 3
Follow the lines and copy each word.

them — the
the — shed
ring — fish
shed — than
than — them
fish — ring

fist — hem
has — sing
hem — them
sing — cast
them — fist
cast — has

Sound/symbol relationships, word completion, copying words

Lesson 24   **27**

Lesson 24

Name _____

Part 4
Circle the sounds.

n m r e n r m o a r t (n) s m t h s (n) i (n) m ⑧
f t m e a t (n) e m s (n) t i h s e r t m o (n)

sh t h i (sh) e i f h (sh) e h f d t h s d t h ⑥
t (sh) e i f h (sh) e f s d f (sh) e t (sh) t

th s h e e (th) f i g h e f (th) i d r i m r ⑤
h r t d t e s n e (th) f m e n (th) s e

Part 5
Read the words and sentences.

them   sing   ant   fits
mash   not   thin   than
got   fast   seems   cot
teeth   his   sand   she

1. Dad did math.
2. She can see that reef.

☐ ☐ ☐ ☐ ☐ ☐

(Parent's/Listener's) signature _____ Date _____

Directions, Part 5:
1. Tell the student to read each row of words and the sentences.
2. Make a check mark in the box if the student reads all the words in the row or in the sentence correctly.

28   *Lesson 24*

Lesson 25

Name _____

Part 4
Circle the sounds.

e t d f (e) g r i a t r f d g (e) a o i m n th f ⑤
a (e) i n t g h c sh m o f r i (e) a h t th (e)

t (d) t r f e o g h i a f m n e o h g (t) r f e ④
i o n c m f r (t) i s a g n e a m r f (t) r g

a e f g (d) c i m n g f (d) e s a t r f g c i ⑤
(d) m n (d) f r e a s f c e (d) o i c a g r t s

n m s t d f (n) s h o a e r i h th (n) m e r f t ④
o t c i m (n) r e o f g sh t th i a c d (n) r

Part 5
Read the words and sentences.

need   mad   fin   not ⬆
ant   sing   feet   mist ⬆
is   mod   has   if ⬆
sand   than   shin   got ⬆

1. That dash is fast.

2. He has rats and cats.

☐ ☐ ☐ ☐ ☐ ☐

(Parent's/Listener's) signature _____ **Date** _____

Directions, Part 5:
1. Tell the student to read each row of words and the sentences.
2. Make a check mark in the box if the student reads all the words in the row or in the sentence correctly.

30   *Lesson 25*

Copyright © SRA/McGraw-Hill. Permission is granted to reproduce for classroom use.

Lesson 25

Name _____

Part 1
Write in the missing letters.

ring _____ *than*
meets _____ *ring*
din _____ *meets*
than _____ *din*

Part 2
Follow the lines and copy each sound.

g — _____ *o*
e — _____ *c*
n — _____ *sh*
o — _____ *g*
c — _____ *e*
sh — _____ *n*

shed — _____ *has*
his — _____ *not*
fast — _____ *his*
not — _____ *shed*
feed — _____ *feed*
has — _____ *fast*

Part 3
Follow the lines and copy each word.

ding — _____ *mad*
mad — _____ *meets*
dish — _____ *dish*
meets — _____ *ding*
sham — _____ *got*
got — _____ *sham*

Lesson 25   29

Word completion, sound/symbol relationships, copying words

Copyright © SRA/McGraw-Hill. Permission is granted to reproduce for classroom use.

127

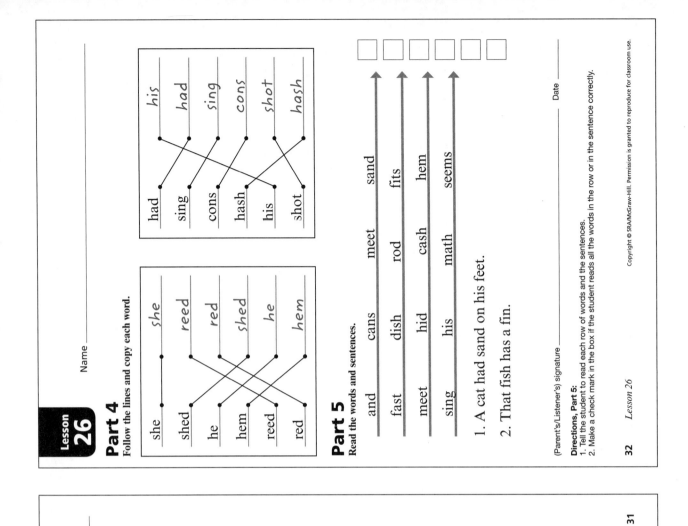

Name

Part 4
Follow the lines and copy each word.

she	_she_
shed	_reed_
he	_red_
hem	_shed_
reed	_he_
red	_hem_

had	_his_
sing	_had_
cons	_sing_
hash	_cons_
his	_shot_
shot	_hash_

Part 5
Read the words and sentences.

☐ ☐ ☐ ☐ ☐ ☐

and	cans	meet	sand
fast	dish	rod	fits
meet	hid	cash	hem
sing	his	math	seems

1. A cat had sand on his feet.

2. That fish has a fin.

(Parent's/Listener's signature) _____ Date _____

Directions, Part 5:
1. Tell the student to read each row of words and the sentences.
2. Make a check mark in the box if the student reads all the words in the row or in the sentence correctly.

32   *Lesson 26*

Copyright © SRA/McGraw-Hill. Permission is granted to reproduce for classroom use.

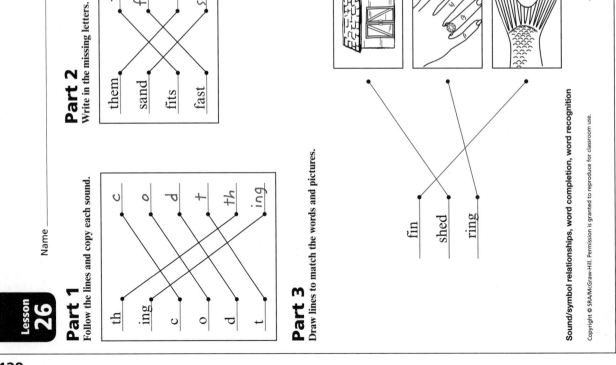

128

Name

Part 1
Follow the lines and copy each sound.

th	_c_
ing	_o_
c	_d_
o	_t_
d	_th_
t	_ing_

Part 2
Write in the missing letters.

them	_fits_
sand	_fast_
fits	_them_
fast	_sand_

Part 3
Draw lines to match the words and pictures.

fin

shed

ring

Sound/symbol relationships, word completion, word recognition

Lesson 26   31

Copyright © SRA/McGraw-Hill. Permission is granted to reproduce for classroom use.

Part 4
Circle the sounds.

g c d t f r i e a f t g c m a s r f c g r f f h ⑤
e a o c i m n g f t d f e g r i a t r f f d g

r m n r a f e c g h i o a r e c d a s t f r ⑥
o e a i n r m c e n o f r i s a h t t h r e

c o a i c r f f g h n m c e d r a s i o f g c ⑤
e f r g i o c d e s a g n e c m r f f t r g i

e d t r f e o g h i a f m n e o h g t r f e ⑤
i o n c m f f r t i s e d o i c a g r t s e m

Part 5
Read the words and sentences.

teen   ten   tan   tin
end   send   mend   sand
hit   hat   hot   that
cash   dash   fast   dish

1. She hid in the hen shed.

2. He met them on the ant hill.

☐ ☐ ☐ ☐ ☐ ☐

(Parent's/Listener's) signature _____ Date _____

Directions, Part 5:
1. Tell the student to read each row of words and the sentences.
2. Make a check mark in the box if the student reads all the words in the row or in the sentence correctly.

34   Lesson 27

Lesson
27

Part 1
Write in the missing letters.

sent _____ mats
mats _____ fast
fast _____ mend
mend _____ sent

Part 2
Follow the lines and copy each sound.

c _____ g
e _____ c
g _____ e
a _____ sh
sh _____ d
d _____ a

sad _____ seed
hit _____ sad
cash _____ math
seed _____ them
math _____ hit
them _____ cash

Part 3
Follow the lines and copy each word.

hot _____ tin
ring _____ ten
ten _____ hot
sod _____ ring
teen _____ teen
tin _____ sod

Word completion, sound/symbol relationships, copying words

Lesson 27   33

130

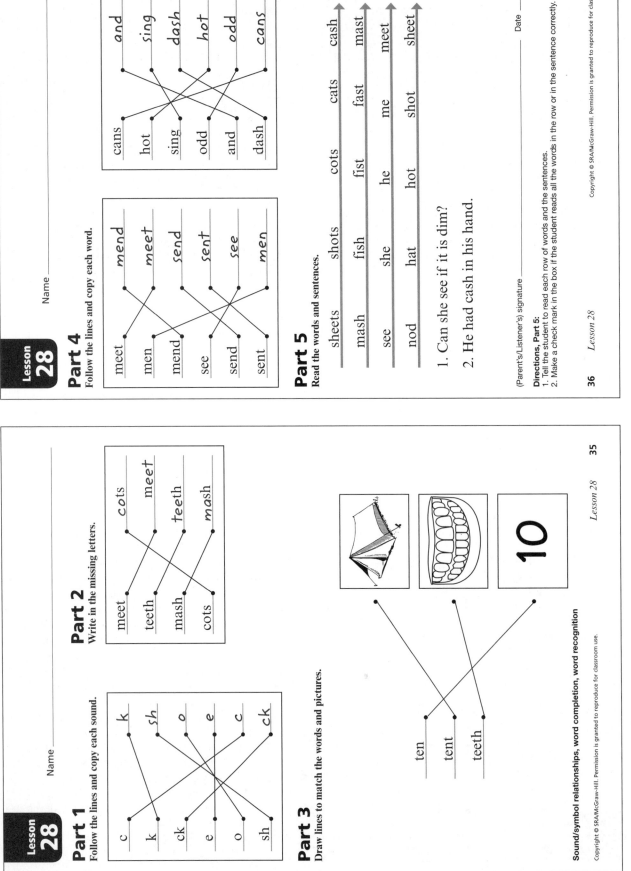

Lesson 28

Part 1
Follow the lines and copy each sound.

c — k
k — k
ck — sh
e — o
o — e
sh — c
— ck

Part 2
Write in the missing letters.

meet — cots
teeth — meet
mash — teeth
cots — mash

Part 3
Draw lines to match the words and pictures.

ten
tent
teeth

10

Lesson 28   35

Sound/symbol relationships, word completion, word recognition

Copyright © SRA/McGraw-Hill. Permission is granted to reproduce for classroom use.

Lesson 28

Name _____

Part 4
Follow the lines and copy each word.

meet — mend
men — meet
mend — send
see — sent
send — see
sent — men

cans — and
hot — sing
sing — dash
odd — hot
and — odd
dash — cans

Part 5
Read the words and sentences.

sheets   shots   cots   cats   cash
mash   fish   fist   fast   mast
see   she   he   me   meet
nod   hat   hot   shot   sheet

☐ ☐ ☐ ☐ ☐ ☐

1. Can she see if it is dim?

2. He had cash in his hand.

_____   _____
(Parent's/Listener's signature)   Date

Directions, Part 5:
1. Tell the student to read each row of words and the sentences.
2. Make a check mark in the box if the student reads all the words in the row or in the sentence correctly.

36   Lesson 28

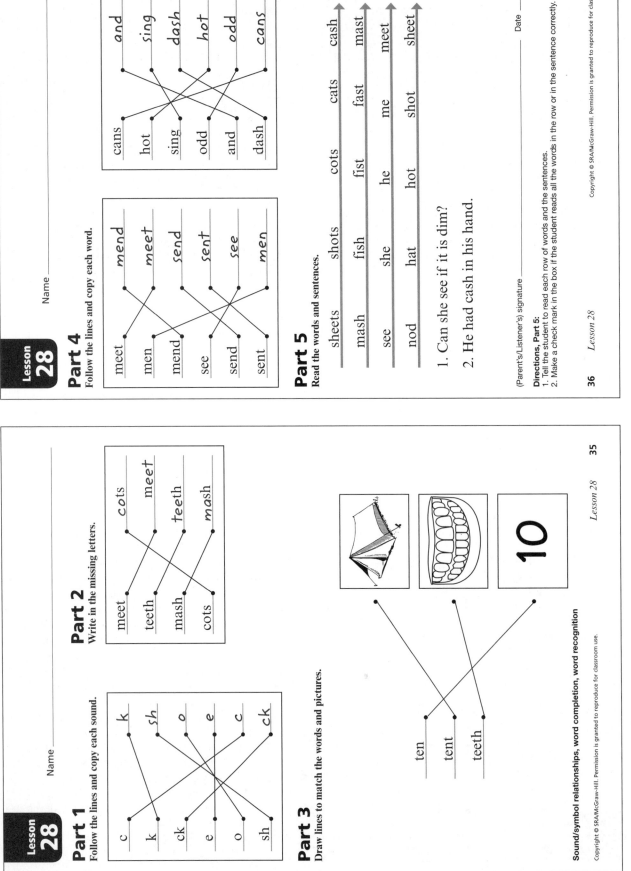

Copyright © SRA/McGraw-Hill. Permission is granted to reproduce for classroom use.

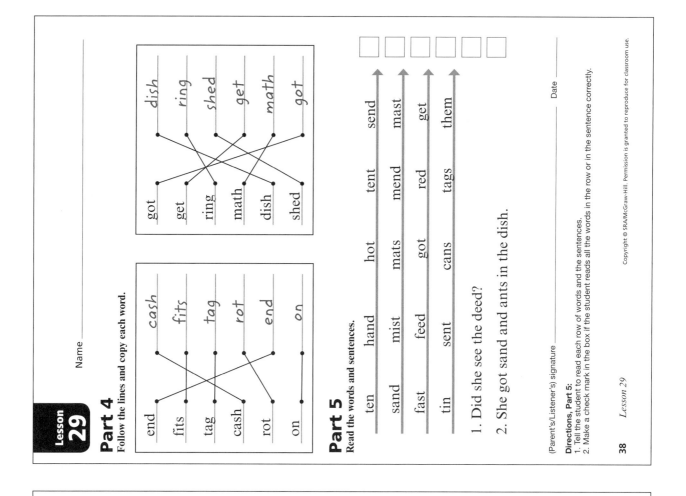

Lesson 29

Part 1
Circle the sounds.

k g f t r d **k** s a r m n i o t h g r **r** **k** o i r
e d **k** s i o **k** n m d e f g h **k** i o m **k** n
a r e t g h i o m n **k** d f g **k** o i r e m h

h d t r f e o g **h** i a f m n e o **h** g t r f a
i o n **h** f r t i s m s t d **h** c s o a **h** i
h f n m e **h** f t g o t c i m n **h** e o i d e

t a g n e c m r f t **t** r g i n m c a d t s a f
t c m n a d **h** t f m n r a f **t** c g h i o a
e c d a s t f g r o e a **t** i r m c e r h o

i a s d f **i** h k g o r e m n c d f f g h k **i** o
d a s m n c d f **i** e g h **i** k a e d r o e s
n c r **i** s a o e d f r **i** o a **i** f g h t a m

⑧

⑧

⑦

⑦

Part 2
Write in the missing letters.

mast — — sent

shots — — tin

tin — — shots

sent — — mast

Part 3
Follow the lines and copy each sound.

c — — ck

ck — — e

g — — n

e — — sh

sh — — c

n — — g

Sound/symbol relationships, word completion

Copyright © SRA/McGraw-Hill. Permission is granted to reproduce for classroom use.

Lesson 29   37

Lesson 29

Name _____

Part 4
Follow the lines and copy each word.

end — — dish

fits — — ring

tag — — shed

cash — — get

rot — — math

on — — got

got — — cash

get — — fits

ring — — tag

math — — rot

dish — — end

shed — — on

Part 5
Read the words and sentences.

☐ ☐ ☐ ☐ ☐ ☐

ten	hand	hot	tent	send
sand	mist	mats	mend	mast →
fast	feed	got	red	get →
tin	sent	cans	tags	them →

1. Did she see the deed?

2. She got sand and ants in the dish.

(Parent's/Listener's) signature _____   Date _____

38   *Lesson 29*

Copyright © SRA/McGraw-Hill. Permission is granted to reproduce for classroom use.

Lesson 30

Name _____

Part 1
Follow the lines and copy each sound.

ing — ck
th — c
r — k
c — r
k — ing
ck — th

Part 2
Write in the missing letters.

hand — tags
tags — fist
fist — tree
tree — hand

Part 3
Follow the lines and copy each word.

not — cans
ten — not
cans — ten
he — hits
hits — meet
meet — he

rag
has
socks
if
sing
odd

if
rag
odd
sing
has
socks

Sound/symbol relationships, word completion, copying words

Lesson 30   **39**

Lesson 30

Name _____

Part 4
Circle the sounds.

d s e m ⓓ c t a s m e ⓓ t s a c h ⓓ e ⓓ
a e ⓓ o m ⓓ e m s t f e ⓓ a h ⓓ f e ⑧

g m e i ⓖ a l c s ⓖ e m r s e ⓖ l o r ⑦
ⓖ i l e ⓖ r e l s c e ⓖ r ⓖ e m h a

ⓒⓚ i t m ⓒⓚ e th i s e i d ⓒⓚ t e i ⓒⓚ e ⑥
ⓒⓚ d e i t m ⓒⓚ i e th ⓒⓚ i e th sh

Part 5
Read the words and sentences.

fig	add	get	tin	shots
tent	cans	men	teeth	nod
ant	hot	dash	his	fish
leg	then	them	sacks	fits

1. An ant is not fast in the dash.

2. Did he get mad at his cats?

☐ ☐ ☐ ☐ ☐ ☐

(Parent's/Listener's) signature _____   Date _____

40   *Lesson 30*

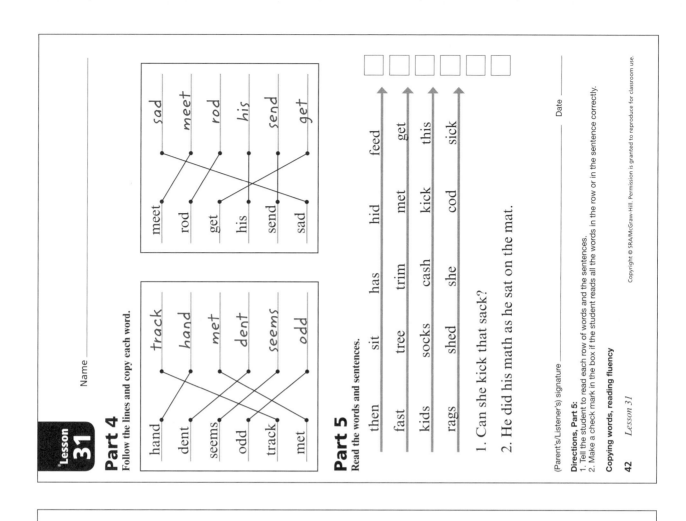

Lesson 31

Name _____

Part 1
Write in the missing letters.

sacks	_dent_
dent	_sacks_
cans	_shots_
shots	_cans_

Part 2
Follow the lines and copy each sound.

c	_ck_
k	_sh_
ck	_k_
sh	_c_
th	_r_
r	_th_

Part 3
Draw lines to match the words and pictures.

rocks

socks

sacks

Word completion, sound/symbol relationships, word recognition

Copyright © SRA/McGraw-Hill. Permission is granted to reproduce for classroom use.

Lesson 31   **41**

Lesson 31

Name _____

Part 4
Follow the lines and copy each word.

hand	_track_
dent	_hand_
seems	_met_
odd	_dent_
track	_seems_
met	_odd_

meet	_sad_
rod	_meet_
get	_rod_
his	_his_
send	_send_
sad	_get_

Part 5
Read the words and sentences.

then	sit	has	hid	feed	☐
fast	tree	trim	met	get	☐
kids	socks	cash	kick	this	☐
rags	shed	she	cod	sick	☐

1. Can she kick that sack? ☐

2. He did his math as he sat on the mat. ☐

(Parent's/Listener's) signature _____ Date _____

Directions, Part 5:
1. Tell the student to read each row of words and the sentences.
2. Make a check mark in the box if the student reads all the words in the row or in the sentence correctly.

Copying words, reading fluency

42   *Lesson 31*

Copyright © SRA/McGraw-Hill. Permission is granted to reproduce for classroom use.

133

Lesson 32

Name _____

Part 1
Follow the lines and copy each sound.

w	wh
wh	w
ck	ing
k	ck
c	g
g	k
ing	c

Part 2
Write in the missing letters.

rags	trot
fits	rags
rocks	fits
trot	rocks

Part 3
Draw lines to match the words and pictures.

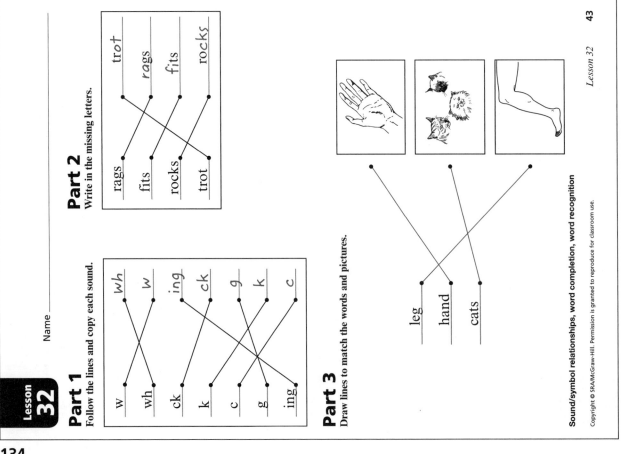

leg

hand

cats

Lesson 32   43

Lesson 32

Name _____

Part 4
Follow the lines and copy each word.

than	had
win	feed
had	on
feed	win
on	cans
cans	than

seems	mend
them	sheets
fish	them
sheets	seems
hid	hid
mend	fish

☐ ☐ ☐ ☐ ☐ ☐

Part 5
Read the words and sentences.

did   dad   not   had   then

week   his   that   street   how

kicks   needs   ring   end   got

if   and   send   teen   rocks

1. Did she get a cast on the leg?

2. Can she sit and fish in the mist?

(Parent's/Listener's) signature _____   Date _____

Directions, Part 5:
1. Tell the student to read each row of words and the sentences.
2. Make a check mark in the box if the student reads all the words in the row or in the sentence correctly.

44   *Lesson 32*

Part 4
Follow the lines and copy each word.

cans	trot
sing	cans
when	sing
trot	hits
hits	red
red	when

that	did
did	fast
mash	that
fast	send
send	has
has	mash

☐ ☐ ☐ ☐ ☐ ☐

Part 5
Read the words and sentences.

we	when	wheel	with	this
sad	kick	dash	go	street
go	singing	tree	week	feed
sheets	shots	hot	how	hands

1. Did sand get in the street?

2. She did not see him.

(Parent's/Listener's) signature _____ Date _____

Directions, Part 5:
1. Tell the student to read each row of words and the sentences.
2. Make a check mark in the box if the student reads all the words in the row or in the sentence correctly.

Part 1
Write in the missing letters.

when	than
than	tree
tree	mast
mast	when

Part 2
Follow the lines and copy each sound.

w	k
c	w
k	c
g	g
t	f
f	t

Part 3
Draw lines to match the words and pictures.

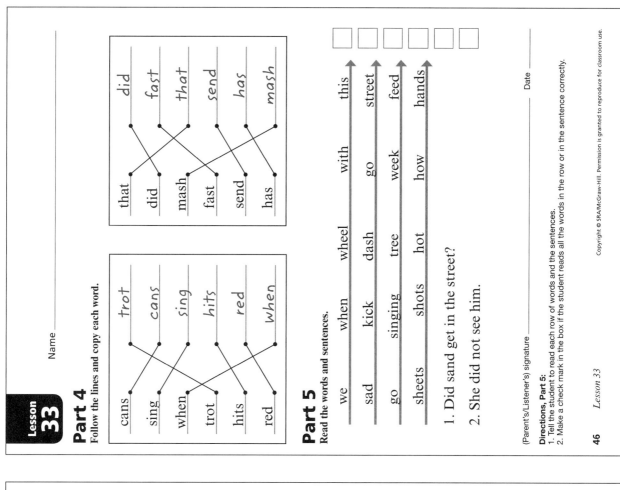

ring

wheel

hot

Word completion, sound/symbol relationships, word recognition

Lesson 34

Name _____

Part 1
Follow the lines and copy each sound.

a
e
i
wh
w
c

i
w
a
c
wh
e

Part 2
Write in the missing letters.

cash — _mend_
mend — _dots_
dots — _needs_
needs — _cash_

Part 3
Draw lines to match the words and pictures.

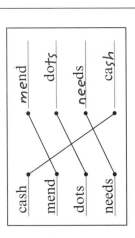

tree
men
hen

Sound/symbol relationships, word completion, word recognition

Lesson 34   **47**

Lesson 34

Name _____

Part 4
Circle the words.

his — a t i f o n i n (his) h a s m e e t r e s e e (his) n o t (his) t h e d i s h f i s h a n d n o d (his) o d d t h e n w h e n (his) m a t h c o d (his) f ⑥

at — h i t s h e r o c k (at) m e t r i n g o o n (at) a m h e m e s e e m (at) j i n m a d s i t (at) s o c k h i s m a s h (at) f a s t w i t h (at) s e e w i n (at) ⑦

miss — m a s s r e e m s s a m (miss) m i t t f e e d r i (miss) m i s s r m e e t (miss) m a s s r e e m m a s t (miss) m i s t m e f e e t (miss) ⑤

Part 5
Read the words and sentences.

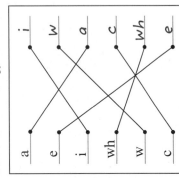

no   not   got   go   get

had   hand   sent   cans   cast

trot   tree   street   wheel   we

ring   ringing   with   math   mash

1. Can she see when it is dim?

2. His fat fish is not fast.

(Parent's/Listener's) signature _____   Date _____

Directions, Part 5:
1. Tell the student to read each row of words and the sentences.
2. Make a check mark in the box if the student reads all the words in the row or in the sentence correctly.

48   *Lesson 34*

Name _____

Part 1
Write in the missing letters.

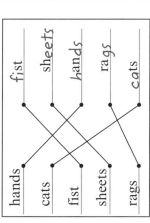

hands ____ fist
cats ____ sheets
fist ____ hands
sheets ____ rags
rags ____ cats

Part 2
Follow the lines and copy each sound.

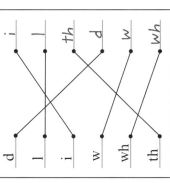

d ____ i
l ____ l
i ____ th
w ____ d
wh ____ w
th ____ wh

Part 3
Circle the words.

met a t h e m e s e **met** m a d r a **met** e t **met** w e t s a m s e **met** s
she m e **met** m i s s r e e m s a c k **met** m i s s c a m s c a s t **met** t s   ⑥

on i n a s a m r a m **on** i n i s h o t r o d **on** g o t g e t i t i n **on** i f i s
g o f a s t i f **on** h o t g e t **on** j s a s a m m a d **on** i f i n **on** m e e   ⑦

sad s e e d s i d s e e **sad** s i c k h a d m a d **sad** r i d r o d h i d h a
m a d o n i f **sad** s a c k s e e m r e e f a s a m **sad** s o c k s o **sad**   ⑤

Word completion, sound/symbol relationships, word matching

Lesson 35   49

Name _____

Part 4
Follow the lines and copy each word.

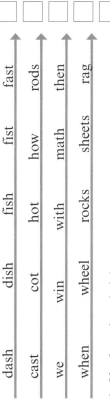

hash ____ tags
shed ____ tent
fits ____ shed
nods ____ hash
tent ____ nods
tags ____ fits

deeds ____ cots
hams ____ met
met ____ deeds
them ____ end
end ____ hams
cots ____ them

Part 5
Read the words and sentences.

dash	dish	fish	fist	fast
cast	cot	hot	how	rods
we	win	with	math	then
when	wheel	rocks	sheets	rag

☐ ☐ ☐ ☐ ☐ ☐

1. She is sad and sick.

2. When did the man feed his cats?

_____ (Parent's/Listener's) signature   Date _____

Directions, Part 5:
1. Tell the student to read each row of words and the sentences.
2. Make a check mark in the box if the student reads all the words in the row or in the sentence correctly.

50   *Lesson 35*

138

Name _____

Part 1
Follow the lines and copy each sound.

l   l

i   ck

k   k

c   c

ck   wh

wh   th

th   i

Part 2
Write in the missing letters.

when   track

will   well

than   when

track   will

well   than

Part 3
Draw lines to match the words and pictures.

sick

sock

lock

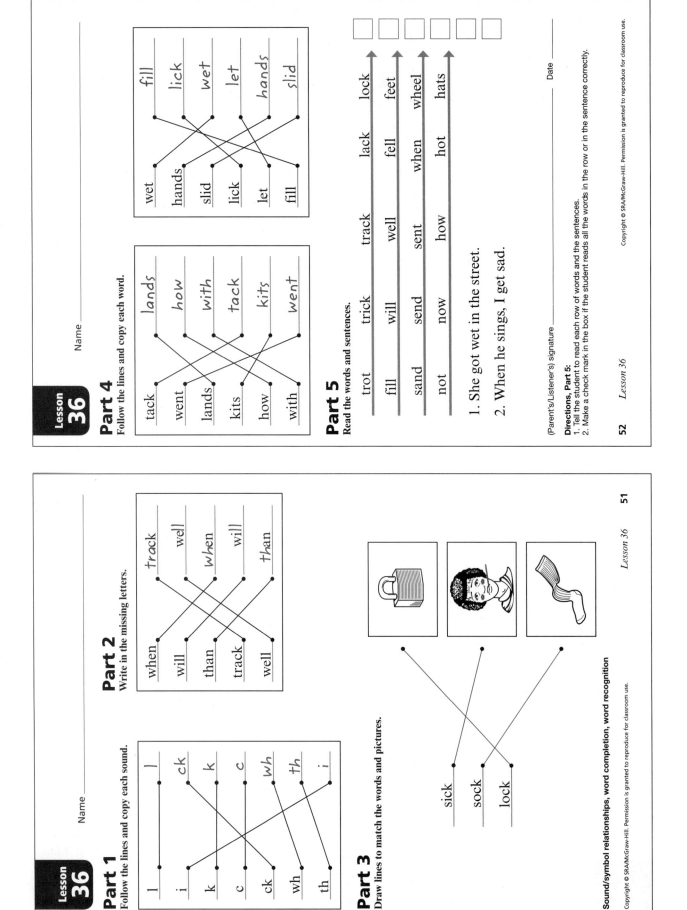

Sound/symbol relationships, word completion, word recognition

Copyright © SRA/McGraw-Hill. Permission is granted to reproduce for classroom use.

Lesson 36   **51**

Name _____

Part 4
Follow the lines and copy each word.

tack   lands

went   how

lands   with

kits   tack

how   kits

with   went

wet   fill

hands   lick

slid   wet

lick   let

let   hands

fill   slid

Part 5
Read the words and sentences.

trot   trick   track   lack   lock

fill   will   well   fell   feet

sand   send   sent   when   wheel

not   now   how   hot   hats

☐ ☐ ☐ ☐ ☐ ☐

1. She got wet in the street.

2. When he sings, I get sad.

_____   _____
(Parent's/Listener's) signature   Date

Directions, Part 5:
1. Tell the student to read each row of words and the sentences.
2. Make a check mark in the box if the student reads all the words in the row or in the sentence correctly.

52   *Lesson 36*

Copyright © SRA/McGraw-Hill. Permission is granted to reproduce for classroom use.

Lesson 37

Part 1
Write in the missing letters.

cold — socks
socks — kits
kits — cold
hands — well
well — hands

Part 2
Follow the lines and copy each sound.

ol — l
l — ol
i — r
r — i
er — w
w — er

Part 3
Circle the words.

(it) i s i s o n o n (it) a n t t h a t s e e m (it) i f i s o n h e h a s (it) f a s t o n (it) i
n o t n o d t h e (it) i n i s o n w e t g o t f i n w i n (it) f i o n t r i m (it) f i   ⑦

(the) t h a t t h a n (the) t h i s (the) t h a n t r e e t e e a g s (the) a t (the) a t (the) a t
t r a c k (the) t h a t t r i c k (the) t h i s t a c k (the) t h e t a n (the) t e n t h   ⑧

(fit) f i s t f a s t f i n s (fit) f i g s f i s h f i l l (fit) (fit) f i s t f a t (fit) f i s t f a t (fit) f i s t f i
s h f (fit) f i n f e l l (fit) f i l l (fit) f i n f a n f a s t (fit) f i s t f i l l f i n (fit) f i t f a s t   ⑦

Word completion, sound/symbol relationships, word matching

Copyright © SRA/McGraw-Hill. Permission is granted to reproduce for classroom use.

Lesson 37   53

Lesson 37

Part 4
Follow the lines and copy each word.

clam — crack
crack — how
sleek — shed
mills — clam
shed — mills
how — sleek

went — lend
slam — got
with — with
got — track
lend — slam
track — went

Part 5
Read the words and sentences.

get	got	rags	gas	cats
trim	trees	street	send	hands
sacks	lick	click	lack	lands
wet	went	will	wheel	when

1. That wheel has wet sand on it.

2. I did not see that shell.

(Parent's/Listener's) signature _____ Date _____

Directions, Part 5:
1. Tell the student to read each row of words and the sentences.
2. Make a check mark in the box if the student reads all the words in the row or in the sentence correctly.

54   *Lesson 37*

Copyright © SRA/McGraw-Hill. Permission is granted to reproduce for classroom use.

139

Part 4
Follow the lines and copy each word.

mist —— tells

class —— mist

tells —— class

kits —— tree

hot —— hot

tree —— kits

cold —— cats

last —— went

clock —— will

went —— cold

cats —— last

will —— clock

Part 5
Read the words and sentences.

cold	sold	sled	slam	land
lend	lack	cracks	shack	shell
street	sell	tells	slim	hill
has	hold	how	her	letter

1. Ten cats did not feel well.

2. She slid her sled on the hill.

(Parent's/Listener's) signature _____ Date _____

Directions, Part 5:
1. Tell the student to read each row of words and the sentences.
2. Make a check mark in the box if the student reads all the words in the row or in the sentence correctly.

Part 1
Follow the lines and copy each sound.

er —— i

ol —— l

i —— wh

l —— er

wh —— ck

ck —— ol

Part 2
Write in the missing letters.

mint —— tree

sold —— sled

tree —— shell

sled —— mint

shell —— sold

Part 3
Circle the sentence that tells about the picture.

This wheel has a track in it.

(This wheel has a tack in it.)

This wheel has a rack on it.

Directions, Part 3: Read the directions to the student: *Circle the sentence that tells about the picture.*

Part 1
Write in the missing letters.

lock — wish
sleek — clam
hold — lock
wish — sleek
clam — hold

Part 2
Follow the lines and copy each sound.

p — g
g — k
ing — d
d — ing
k — n
n — p

Part 3
Circle the sentence that tells about the picture.

He has a cat in his hand.

He has a rat in his hand.

(He has an ant in his hand.)

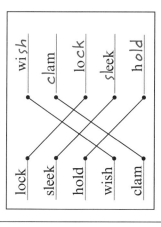

Part 4
Follow the lines and copy each word.

sell — this
shop — sell
this — pet
last — now
pet — last
now — shop

hot — cold
cold — socks
clap — hot
wish — fast
socks — wish
fast — clap

Part 5
Read the words and sentences.

this	than	then	when	well
fell	tells	sad	sadder	how
will	win	winner	lip	slip
last	list	land	pet	pit

☐ ☐ ☐ ☐ ☐ ☐

1. How well can she sing?

2. If it is not hot, we will sleep.

(Parent's/Listener's) signature _____ Date _____

Directions, Part 5:
1. Tell the student to read each row of words and the sentences.
2. Make a check mark in the box if the student reads all the words in the row or in the sentence correctly.

141

142

Lesson 40

Name _____

Part 1
Follow the lines and copy each sound.

wh — w
w — wh
th — ol
p — th
ol — er
er — p

Part 2
Write in the missing letters.

shops — cast
send — cats
trim — trim
cats — send
cast — shops

Part 3
Draw lines to match the words and pictures.

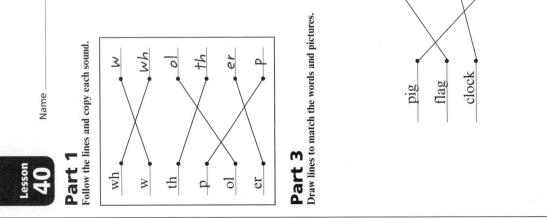

pig
flag
clock

Sound/symbol relationships, word completion, word recognition

Copyright © SRA/McGraw-Hill. Permission is granted to reproduce for classroom use.

Lesson 40   59

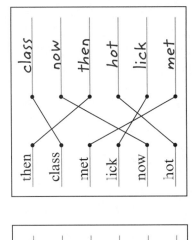

Lesson 40

Name _____

Part 4
Follow the lines and copy each word.

meet — class
last — now
tracks — then
how — hot
down — lick
went — met

then — class
class — now
met — then
lick — hot
now — lick
hot — met

Part 5
Read the words and sentences.

☐ ☐ ☐ ☐ ☐ ☐

pig   pet   petting   tack
sing   singer   letter   pack   how
has   hats   hand   think   lend
lip   slip   sleep   lands   tree
                  sheep

1. That cat is slim and sleek.

2. How fast can he go with that cast?

(Parent's/Listener's signature) _____ Date _____

Directions, Part 5:
1. Tell the student to read each row of words and the sentences.
2. Make a check mark in the box if the student reads all the words in the row or in the sentence correctly.

60   *Lesson 40*

Copyright © SRA/McGraw-Hill. Permission is granted to reproduce for classroom use.

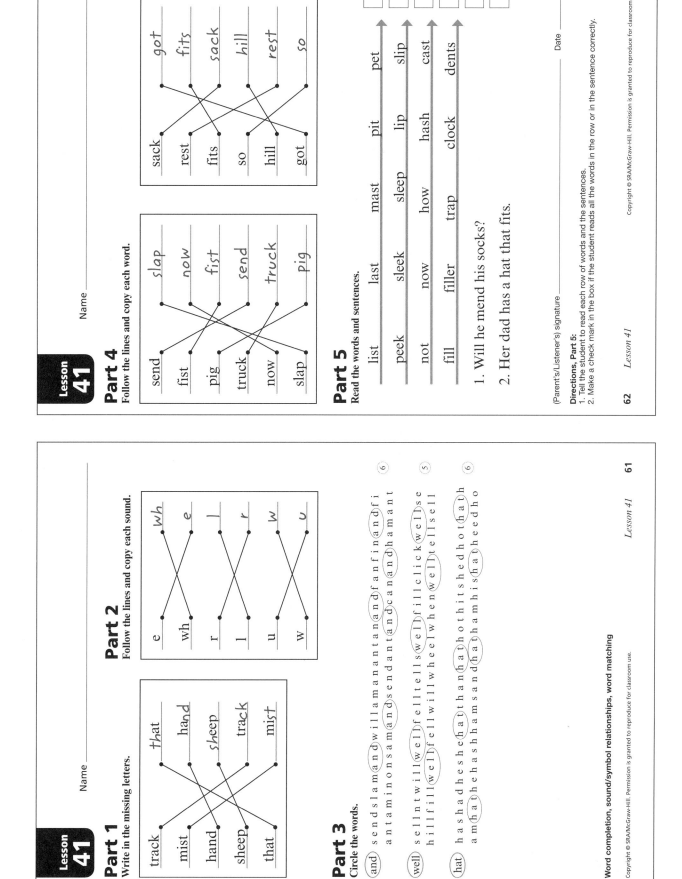

Lesson 41

Name _____

Part 1
Write in the missing letters.

track — *that*
mist — *hand*
hand — *sheep*
sheep — *track*
that — *mist*

Part 2
Follow the lines and copy each sound.

e — *wh*
wh — *e*
r — *l*
l — *r*
u — *w*
w — *u*

Part 3
Circle the words.

(and) s e n d s l a m (and) w i l l a m a n a n t a n (and) f a n f i n (and) f i
a n t a m i n o n s a m (and) s e n d a n t (and) c a n a n (and) h a m a n t ⑥

(well) s e l l n t w i l l (well) f e l l t e l l s (well) f i l l c l i c k (well) s e ⑤
h i l l f i l l (well) f e l l w i l l w h e e l w h e n (well) t e l l s e l l

(hat) h a s h a d h e s h e (hat) h a t h (hat) h o t h i t s h e d h o t (hat) h a t h ⑥
a m (hat) h e h a s h h a m s h (hat) h a m h i s (hat) h e e d h o

Word completion, sound/symbol relationships, word matching

Lesson 41 **61**

Lesson 41

Name _____

Part 4
Follow the lines and copy each word.

send — *slap*
fist — *now*
pig — *fist*
truck — *send*
now — *truck*
slap — *pig*

sack — *got*
rest — *fits*
fits — *sack*
so — *hill*
hill — *rest*
got — *so*

Part 5
Read the words and sentences.

list	last	mast	pit	pet
peek	sleek	sleep	lip	slip
not	now	how	hash	cast
fill	filler	trap	clock	dents

☐ ☐ ☐ ☐ ☐ ☐

1. Will he mend his socks?

2. Her dad has a hat that fits.

(Parent's/Listener's) signature _____ Date _____

Directions, Part 5:
1. Tell the student to read each row of words and the sentences.
2. Make a check mark in the box if the student reads all the words in the row or in the sentence correctly.

62 *Lesson 41*

143

Lesson 42

Name _____

Part 1
Follow the lines and copy each sound.

th
ck
x
a
u
ol

ol
a
u
th
ck
x

Part 2
Write in the missing letters.

fast
slim
trees
sheets
shots

sheets
shots
fast
slim
trees

Part 3
Circle the sentence that tells about the picture.

Her hand is on her pet pig.

(The hat is on her pet pig.)

Her pet pig is on the hat.

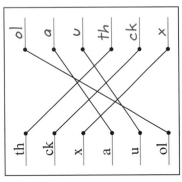

Lesson 42

Lesson 42

Name _____

Part 4
Follow the lines and copy each word.

rust
steep
fish
lock
class
when

steep
class
lock
rust
when
fish

cold
truck
lick
well
then
how

truck
then
lick
cold
how
well

Part 5
Read the words and sentences.

☐ ☐ ☐ ☐ ☐ ☐ ☐

send   sender   sending   rest   last

fold   up   under   stop   truck

step   stem   sleds   clam   crash

fins   fishing   mud   pots   dug

1. I sent her a clock last week.

2. That singer will sing at the dinner.

3. The winner got a gold ring.

(Parent's/Listener's) signature _____ Date _____

Directions, Part 5:
1. Tell the student to read each row of words and the sentences.
2. Make a check mark in the box if the student reads all the words in the row or in the sentence correctly.

Lesson 42

Lesson 43

Part 1
Write in the missing letters.

lock   picks
truck   sleep
under   truck
sleep   under
picks   lock

Part 2
Follow the lines and copy each sound.

or   u
ol   er
er   wh
wh   or
u   p
p   ol

Part 3
Circle the sentence that tells about the picture.

She has a lock in her hand.

She has a cast on her hand.

(She has a clock in her hand.)

Word completion, sound/symbol relationships, sentence reading

145

Name _____

Part 4
Follow the lines and copy each word.

land   hill
slip   when
tent   slip
hill   packs
packs   land
when   tent

must   track
clap   dig
how   her
track   must
dig   how
her   clap

Part 5
Read the words and sentences.

rocks	rocking	locks	list	lip			
went	win	winning	sending	sand			
slap	clap	click	trick	tracks			
ran	run	sings	thing	this			

1. Meet me on the hill.

2. He has a cast on his leg.

3. How will we get dinner on this ship?

(Parent's/Listener's) signature _____ Date _____

Directions, Part 5:
1. Tell the student to read each row of words and the sentences.
2. Make a check mark in the box if the student reads all the words in the row or in the sentence correctly.

Lesson 44

Name _____

Part 1
Follow the lines and copy each sound.

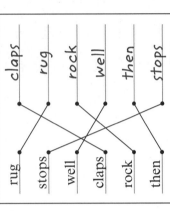

d — u
p — ing
g — n
ing — d
n — p
u — g

Part 2
Write in the missing letters.

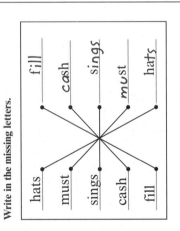

hats — fill
must — cash
sings — sings
cash — must
fill — hats

Part 3
Circle the words.

then — w h e n w i l l w e n t t h i s (then) w e e k s l e e k t h a t (then) t h i
w e l l w h e n (then) t h a t w h e e l (then) t h i s t h a t t h e w h e n   ④

not — n o w h o w h o t (not) s t o p s o c k (not) t h a n t a n n e e d (not) t s
o n i t h o t (not) p o t s n o g o n o (not) h o t r o t r o d h o w (not) h n o w   ⑥

fast — c a s h f i s h (fast) f i s t m a s h m i s t (fast) c a s t c a n
f i n s f i g s f a d d a s h (fast) c a s t m i s t f i s h f e l l (fast) f   ④

Sound/symbol relationships, word completion, word matching

Lesson 44   67

Lesson 44

Name _____

Part 4
Follow the lines and copy each word.

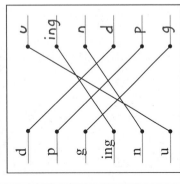

rug — claps
stops — rug
well — rock
claps — well
rock — then
then — stops

drop — steps
will — flag
streets — hand
steps — will
flag — drop
hand — streets

Part 5
Read the words and sentences.

☐ ☐ ☐ ☐ ☐ ☐ ☐ ☐

run   fun   fox   letter   fix   pens   fold
dinner   sadder   sings   sleep   slip   runs
week   must   get   got   sun
mist   dot

1. Send me the clock this week.

2. No man will rent that shack.

3. Stop filling that gas can with sand.

(Parent's/Listener's signature) _____ Date _____

68   Lesson 44

Name _____

Part 4
Follow the lines and copy each word.

and	*or*
but	*now*
or	*told*
now	*and*
big	*big*
told	*but*

when	*got*
dig	*go*
this	*when*
go	*dig*
got	*track*
track	*this*

Part 5
Read the words and sentences.

☐ ☐ ☐ ☐ ☐ ☐ ☐

clap	claps	clapping	street	picks
or	form	torn	must	fell
but	bug	big	dig	dug
pins	peel	told	tag	flags

1. The old man fell on the dock and got wet.

2. She will sing for the class.

3. His socks fit, but his hat is big.

_____ Date _____
(Parent's/Listener's) signature

Directions, Part 5:
1. Tell the student to read each row of words and the sentences.
2. Make a check mark in the box if the student reads all the words in the row or in the sentence correctly.

Name _____

Part 1
Write in the missing letters.

sleep	pe_n_s
pens	flag
flag	ru_n_s
runs	trap
trap	sleep

Part 2
Follow the lines and copy each sound.

t	d
k	p
p	t
d	ol
ol	l
l	k

Part 3
Circle the sentence that tells about the picture.

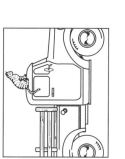

(The cat sat on the truck.) ← circled

The fish sat on the truck.

The cat sat on the fish.

Word completion, sound/symbol relationships, sentence reading

147

148

Lesson 46

Name _____

Part 1
Follow the lines and copy each sound.

p — ol
d — p
f — or
ol — er
or — d
er — f

Part 2
Write in the missing letters.

clock — trees
cuts — clock
street — cuts
hand — hand
trees — street

Part 3
Draw lines to match the words and pictures.

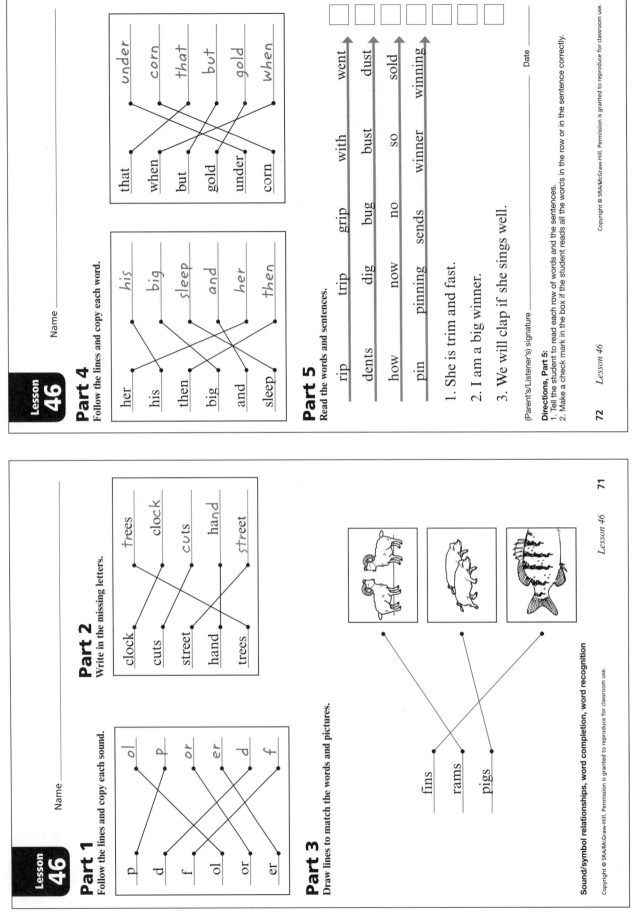

fins
rams
pigs

Sound/symbol relationships, word completion, word recognition

Copyright © SRA/McGraw-Hill. Permission is granted to reproduce for classroom use.

Lesson 46   71

Lesson 46

Name _____

Part 4
Follow the lines and copy each word.

her — his
his — big
then — sleep
big — and
and — her
sleep — then

that — under
when — corn
but — that
gold — but
under — gold
corn — when

Part 5
Read the words and sentences.

rip   trip   grip   with   went
dents   dig   bug   bust   dust
how   now   no   so   sold
pin   pinning   sends   winner   winning

□ □ □ □ □ □ □

1. She is trim and fast.

2. I am a big winner.

3. We will clap if she sings well.

(Parent's/Listener's signature) _____ Date _____

Directions, Part 5:
1. Tell the student to read each row of words and the sentences.
2. Make a check mark in the box if the student reads all the words in the row or in the sentence correctly.

72   Lesson 46

Copyright © SRA/McGraw-Hill. Permission is granted to reproduce for classroom use.

Name _____

Part 4
Follow the lines and copy each word.

told	_red_
cans	_told_
meet	_sits_
rock	_cans_
red	_rock_
sits	_meet_

hits	_sleep_
for	_hats_
when	_for_
sold	_when_
hats	_hits_
sleep	_sold_

Part 5
Read the words and sentences.

corn	born	big	bug	dust
send	sender	finger	pins	pinning
sold	fold	for	horn	how
slip	sheep	shops	stop	swim

□ □ □ □ □ □ □

1. He will lend us his tent.

2. She had dinner with us last week.

3. When did the bell ring?

(Parent's/Listener's signature) _____ Date _____

74   *Lesson 47*

Name _____

Part 1
Write in the missing letters.

hats	_shop_
shop	_green_
green	_hats_
fist	_sick_
sick	_fist_

Part 2
Follow the lines and copy each sound.

ol	_d_
or	_er_
er	_or_
p	_g_
d	_p_
g	_ol_

Part 3
Circle the sentence that tells about the picture.

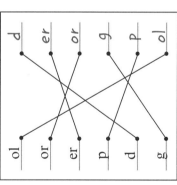

He ran down the steep hill.

He fell down the steep hill.

(He ran up the steep hill.)

Word completion, sound/symbol relationships, sentence reading

Lesson 47   73

Lesson 48

Name _____

Part 1
Follow the lines and copy each sound.

a — p
i — a
x — u
p — x
u — ol
ol — i

Part 2
Draw the lines. Then write in the missing letters.

big — sleep
must — big
sleep — must
track — went
went — track

Part 3
Circle the words.

end   h a n d a n d l (e n d) s a n d s (e n d) p e n s m (e n d) f a n s h a m s a n
      s l e d p e n s p a n s (e n d) s h e d c a n s (e n d) h a n d s s l e d (e n d)   ⑥

his   t h a t t h e t h e (h i s) h a m h i t s h a m t h e t h e n (h i s) h i m h
      h o w h i t (h i s) h i l l s h i n (h i s) w i t h a t w i l l (h i s) h i m h e h i   ⑤

stop s t e p s t e e p s t r e e t (s t o p) p o p s t e p s l i p (s t o p) s l i d s l e
      e k p o t (s t o p) s l p o p (s t o p) s l e d s l e e k (s t o p) s t e p s p o t s   ⑤

when w e t e n d w h e e l w e e k (w h e n) t h a t t h e n w e l l (w h e n) w i
      t h e n w h e n t h a t w e n t w i l l (w h e n) w i n w h e n w h e e l h   ⑤

Directions, Part 2: Read the directions to the student: *Draw the lines. Then write in the missing letters.*

Lesson 48   75

Name _____

Part 4
Follow the lines and copy each word.

this — truck
yell — wish
creek — this
fork — yell
truck — creek
wish — fork

but — cold
cold — short
six — test
happy — but
short — happy
test — six

Part 5
Read the words and sentences.

lack	slack	truck	rugs	crust	☐
slip	fix	shed	silly	happy	☐
yes	bell	bet	fist	land	☐
mix	fox	fits	sold	short	☐

1. Is she swimming in the pond?   ☐

2. The fox is running up the steep hill.   ☐

3. That black colt will trot on the track.   ☐

(Parent's/Listener's) signature _____ Date _____

Directions, Part 5:
1. Tell the student to read each row of words and the sentences.
2. Make a check mark in the box if the student reads all the words in the row or in the sentence correctly.

76   *Lesson 48*

Name _____

Part 1
Draw the lines. Then write in the missing letters.

trip	_lock_
send	_form_
lock	_fast_
form	_trip_
fast	_send_

Part 2
Follow the lines and copy each sound.

u	_er_
r	_y_
h	_u_
sh	_r_
er	_sh_
y	_h_

Part 3
Draw lines to match the words and pictures.

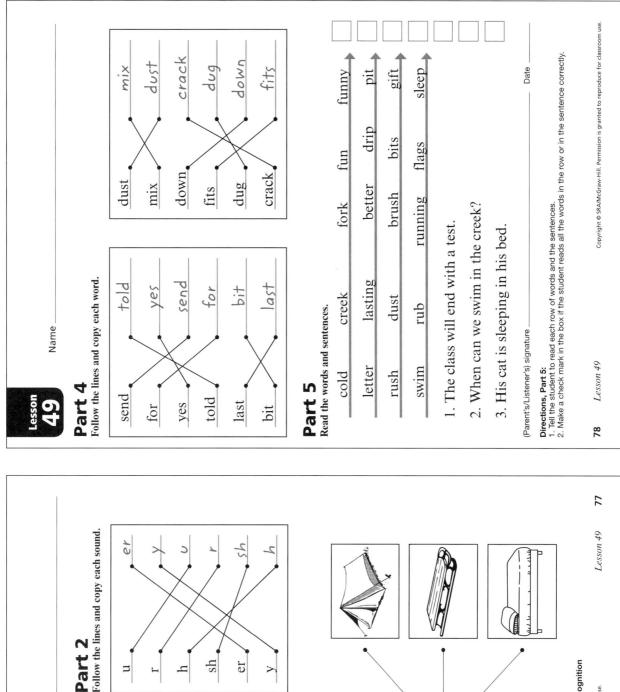

bed
sled
tent

Name _____

Part 4
Follow the lines and copy each word.

send	_told_
for	_yes_
yes	_send_
told	_for_
last	_bit_
bit	_last_

dust	_mix_
mix	_dust_
down	_crack_
fits	_dug_
dug	_down_
crack	_fits_

Part 5
Read the words and sentences.

cold	creek	fork	fun	funny
letter	lasting	better	drip	pit
rush	dust	brush	bits	gift
swim	rub	running	flags	sleep

1. The class will end with a test.

2. When can we swim in the creek?

3. His cat is sleeping in his bed.

(Parent's/Listener's) signature _____ Date _____

Directions, Part 5:
1. Tell the student to read each row of words and the sentences.
2. Make a check mark in the box if the student reads all the words in the row or in the sentence correctly.

78   Lesson 49

Copyright © SRA/McGraw-Hill. Permission is granted to reproduce for classroom use.

152

Name _____

Part 1
Follow the lines and copy each sound.

b — w
f — sh
e — l
sh — b
l — f
w — e

Part 2
Draw the lines. Then write in the missing letters.

born — sack
slip — mist
dug — born
sack — slip
mist — dug

Part 3
Circle the sentence that tells about the picture.

She can not sleep in the short tent.

She can not fit in the short truck.

(She can sleep on the short bed.)

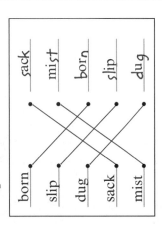

Sound/symbol relationships, word completion, sentence reading

Lesson 50 79

Name _____

Part 4
Follow the lines and copy each word.

sits — rock
then — sits
rock — then

fold — sing
sing — must
must — fold

Part 5
Copy the sentence.
We will go on a trip.
We will go on a trip.

Part 6
Read the words and sentences.

yes	yell	sent	bet	letter
last	slid	flip	flaps	fork
morning	short	best	when	rush
funny	fill	feel	cold	greets

□ □ □ □ □ □

1. See me sleep in the green grass.

2. The math class did not go well.

_____ _____
(Parent's/Listener's signature)   Date

80 *Lesson 50*

Part 1
Draw the lines. Then write in the missing letters.

shops   send
truck   fold
send   shops
dusty   truck
fold   dusty

Part 2
Follow the lines and copy each sound.

n   t
t   f
f   n
ol   er
er   or
or   ol

Part 3
Circle the words.

than the n when thatthtack then (than) this the the the than ④
that th then when the thing (than) this the tack

Part 4
Follow the lines and copy each word.

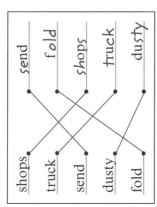

under   fits
grass   got
street   send
got   grass
fits   under
send   street

corn   her
her   corn
fill   but
when   trees
but   when
trees   fill

Word completion, sound/symbol relationships, word matching, copying words

153

Part 5
Copy the sentences.

He will run up the hill.
He will run up the hill.
Her class went to the track meet.
Her class went to the track meet.
The men will sleep in that tent.
The men will sleep in that tent.

Part 6
Read the words and sentences.

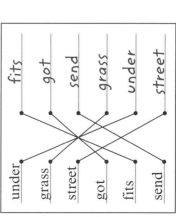

to   is   was   went   wish
cuts   drip   short   felt   fold
yes   hands   smell   steep   drop
black   best   class   dust   green

1. How can he sleep when we sing?

2. That colt trots faster and faster.

3. When they met, they felt happy.

_____ Date _____
(Parent's/Listener's) signature

Lesson 52

Name _____

Part 5
Follow the lines and copy each word.

brush	*hands*
hands	*stop*
stop	*brush*

letter	*creek*
creek	*letter*
short	*short*

Part 6
Copy the sentences.

I will sleep in the green grass.
I will sleep in the green grass.

She went to her swimming class.
She went to her swimming class.

Part 7
Read the words and sentences.

crust	sunny	yet	they	yelling
was	mats	black	gold	much
chip	dropping	six	steps	camp

1. When will they stop sending me letters?

2. The green bug was in that tree.

3. They will lock the shed in the morning.

_____ **Date** _____
(Parent's/Listener's) signature

Directions, Part 7:
1. Tell the student to read each row of words and the sentences.
2. Make a check mark in the box if the student reads all the words in the row or in the sentence correctly.

84   *Lesson 52*

Lesson 52

Name _____

Part 1
Follow the lines and copy each sound.

ch	*ck*
f	*u*
ck	*i*
d	*ch*
i	*f*
u	*d*

Part 2
Draw the lines. Then write in the missing letters.

land	*black*
bugs	*ship*
torn	*land*
ship	*torn*
black	*bugs*

Part 3
Draw lines to match the words and pictures.

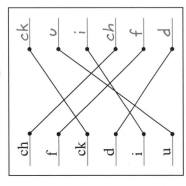

flags

fox

fork

Part 4
Follow the lines and copy each word.

chop	*sing*
luck	*wheel*
bent	*chop*
wheel	*luck*
sing	*fast*
fast	*bent*

Sound/symbol relationships, word completion, word recognition, copying words

Lesson 52   83

154

Lesson 53 — Name _____

Part 1
Draw the lines. Then write in the missing letters.

lamp — lunch
slim — lamp
drops — slim
click — click
lunch — drops

Part 2
Follow the lines and copy each sound.

o — u
r — ck
u — r
ch — o
ck — b
b — ch

Part 3
Circle the sentence that tells about the picture.

The old cat sat on the bed.

(The old cat hid under the bed.)

The old cat sat in the tree.

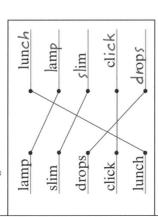

Word completion, sound/symbol relationships, sentence reading

Lesson 53   85

Lesson 53 — Name _____

Part 4
Follow the lines and copy each word.

rugs — still
colder — rugs
still — colder

left — left
cuts — happy
happy — cuts

Part 5
Copy the sentences.

She sat in her truck.
She sat in her truck.

I am happy in this class.
I am happy in this class.

Part 6
Read the words and sentences.

told   to   was   yet   smell
short   shore   store   plant   clip
pan   faster   lend   next   fix

□ □ □ □ □ □

1. They set up a tent at the creek.
2. The pig got in the mud.
3. He sent me a short letter.

(Parent's/Listener's) signature _____ Date _____

Directions, Part 6:
1. Tell the student to read each row of words and the sentences.
2. Make a check mark in the box if the student reads all the words in the row or in the sentence correctly.

86   *Lesson 53*

155

Lesson 54

Name _____

Part 1
Follow the lines and copy each sound.

th — n
ch — ch
n — th

a — or
or — ol
ol — a

Part 2
Draw the lines. Then write in the missing letters.

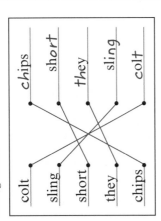

colt — chips
sling — short
short — they
they — sling
chips — colt

Part 3
Circle the words.

(left) l e t l e t t e r l i c k (left) f i l l f l s l e d (left) r e e f b e t t (left)
l e g r e d (left) b e t t e r l e n d (left) e n d t e l l g e t (left) i p l i

Part 4
Follow the lines and copy each word.

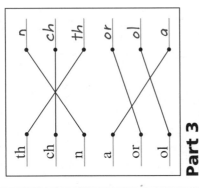

bad — then
sleep — cats
then — dust
cats — sleep
smell — bad
dust — smell

Copyright © SRA/McGraw-Hill. Permission is granted to reproduce for classroom use.

Sound/symbol relationships, word completion, word matching, copying words

---

Lesson 54

Name _____

Part 5
Copy the sentences.

I will go to the store now.
I will go to the store now.

A black cat sat in that tree.
A black cat sat in that tree.

She told me how happy she was.
She told me how happy she was.

Part 6
Read the words and sentences.

bent   dents   dusty   creek   muddy
sore   shore   shops   chop   bath
slams   champ   clamp   block   picking
yelling   still   fold   form   pens

☐ ☐ ☐ ☐ ☐ ☐

1. Next week, we will go on a trip.

2. They had fish and chips for lunch.

3. Did he lock the shed yet?

_____
(Parent's/Listener's) signature   Date

Directions, Part 6:
1. Tell the student to read each row of words and the sentences.
2. Make a check mark in the box if the student reads all the words in the row or or in the sentence correctly.

88   *Lesson 54*

Copyright © SRA/McGraw-Hill. Permission is granted to reproduce for classroom use.

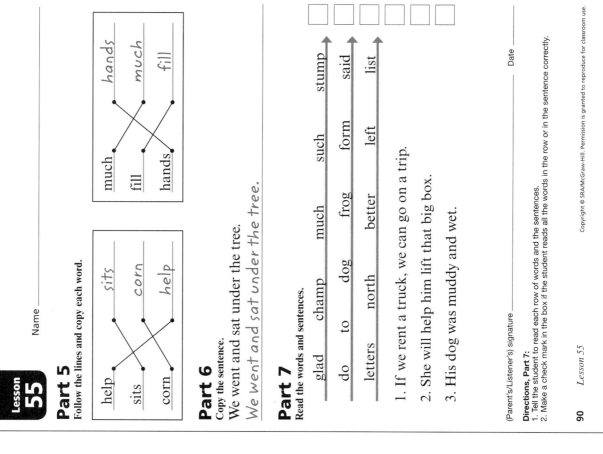

Part 5
Follow the lines and copy each word.

help	sits
sits	corn
corn	help

much	hands
fill	much
hands	fill

Part 6
Copy the sentence.
We went and sat under the tree.
We went and sat under the tree.

Part 7
Read the words and sentences.

glad	champ	much	such	stump
do	to	dog	frog	form	said
letters	north	better	left	list

1. If we rent a truck, we can go on a trip.
2. She will help him lift that big box.
3. His dog was muddy and wet.

(Parent's/Listener's) signature _____ Date _____

Directions, Part 7:
1. Tell the student to read each row of words and the sentences.
2. Make a check mark in the box if the student reads all the words in the row or in the sentence correctly.

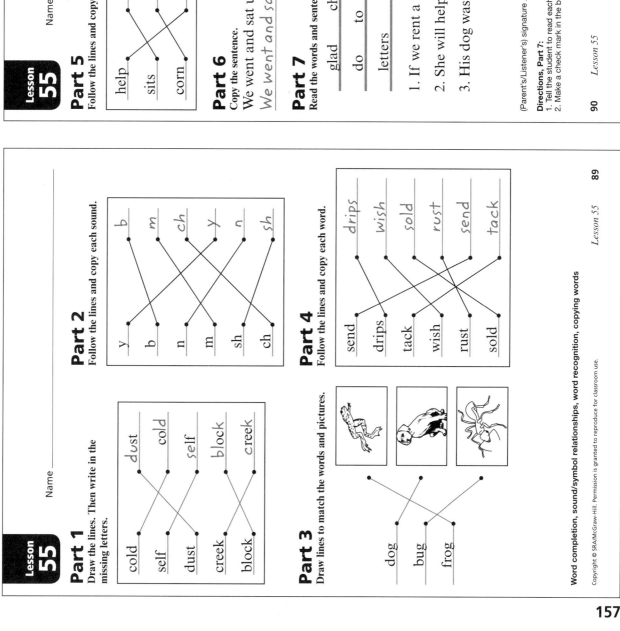

Part 1
Draw the lines. Then write in the missing letters.

cold	dust
self	cold
dust	self
creek	block
block	creek

Part 2
Follow the lines and copy each sound.

y	b
b	m
n	ch
m	y
sh	n
ch	sh

Part 3
Draw lines to match the words and pictures.

dog
bug
frog

Part 4
Follow the lines and copy each word.

send	drips
drips	wish
tack	sold
wish	rust
rust	send
sold	tack

Word completion, sound/symbol relationships, word recognition, copying words

158

Lesson 56

Name _____

Part 1
Follow the lines and copy each sound.

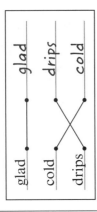

ch _____ th

wh _____ j

th _____ ch

sh _____ w

w _____ wh

j _____ sh

Part 2
Draw the lines. Then write in the missing letters.

flips _____ then

steep _____ town

then _____ stops

town _____ flips

stops _____ steep

Part 3
Circle the sentence that tells about the picture.

(This dog sat in the box.)

This frog sat in the box.

Sound/symbol relationships, word completion, sentence reading

Lesson 56   **91**

Lesson 56

Name _____

Part 4
Follow the lines and copy each word.

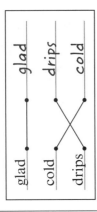

glad _____ glad

cold _____ drips

drips _____ cold

north _____ list

plants _____ plants

list _____ north

Part 5
Copy the sentences.

I can not fix this truck.
I can not fix this truck.

Six men went to the camp.
Six men went to the camp.

Part 6
Read the words and sentences.

jump   jam   plants   stand   still

feel   fell   shelf   down   drops

singer   mister   slips   such   next

☐ ☐ ☐ ☐ ☐ ☐

1. She was the best runner in this town.

2. He said, "Did the cat sleep under the bed?"

3. The tracks led to a shack next to the hill.

(Parent's/Listener's) signature _____   Date _____

Directions, Part 6:
1. Tell the student to read each row of words and the sentences.
2. Make a check mark in the box if the student reads all the words in the row or in the sentence correctly.

92   *Lesson 56*

Name _____

Part 5
Copy the sentences.

We ran up the steep hill.

We ran up the steep hill.

She will get jam at the store.

She will get jam at the store.

Part 6
Follow the lines and copy each word.

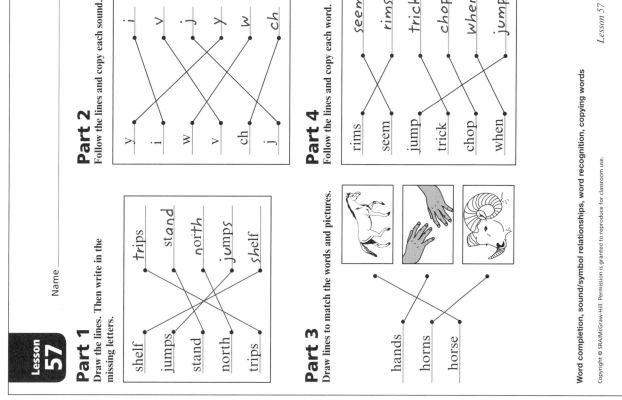

flips	*horse*
mold	*flips*
horse	*mold*

cash	*cash*
pick	*they*
they	*pick*

Part 7
Read the words and sentences.

grab	grin	singer	sending	smell
clamp	champ	chops	tops	stop
job	born	rust	desk	last

1. That plant will fit on this shelf.

2. His dusty dog needs a bath.

3. She ate ham and corn for dinner.

(Parent's/Listener's signature) _____ Date _____

Directions, Part 7:
1. Tell the student to read each row of words and the sentences.
2. Make a check mark in the box if the student reads all the words in the row or in the sentence correctly.

Name _____

Part 1
Draw the lines. Then write in the missing letters.

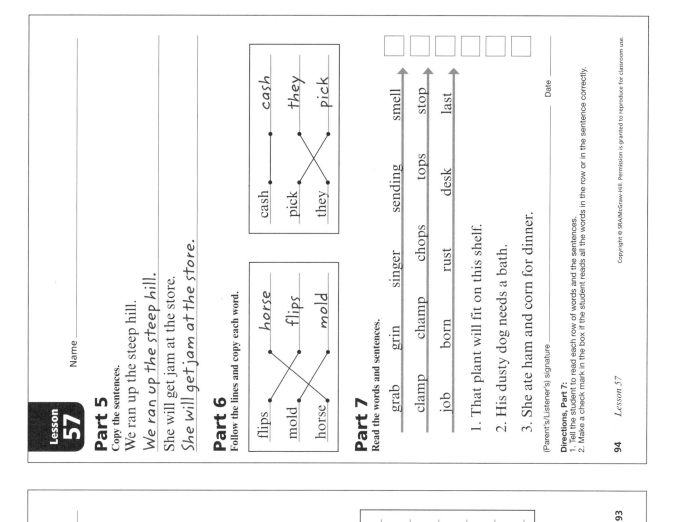

shelf	*trips*
jumps	*stand*
stand	*north*
north	*jumps*
trips	*shelf*

Part 2
Follow the lines and copy each sound.

y	*i*
i	*v*
w	*j*
v	*y*
ch	*w*
j	*ch*

Part 3
Draw lines to match the words and pictures.

hands

horns

horse

Part 4
Follow the lines and copy each word.

rims	*seem*
seem	*rims*
jump	*trick*
trick	*chop*
chop	*when*
when	*jump*

Word completion, sound/symbol relationships, word recognition, copying words

Left Page

Lesson 58

160

Name _____

Part 1
Follow the lines and copy each sound.

d	v
v	d
i	ck
l	or
or	i
ck	l

Part 2
Draw the lines. Then write in the missing letters.

rest	track
track	steep
steep	tops
slips	rest
tops	slips

Part 3
Circle the sentence that tells about the picture.

(The bus went up the street.)

The truck went up the street.

The bus went down the street.

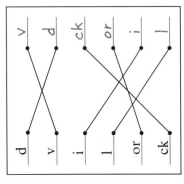

Part 4
Circle the words.

bad   b e s t b i d d a d d b o l t b o r n b i t s (b a d) s a d l a n d (b a d) l a

f a d d a s h (b a d) f a s t m a d p a l (b a d) s a n d f a s t (b a d) b o l d b e t   ⑥

Sound/symbol relationships, word completion, sentence reading, word matching

Lesson 58   95

Right Page

Lesson 58

Name _____

Part 5
Copy the sentences.

The dog sat in the bathtub.

The dog sat in the bathtub.

He got a job at that store.

He got a job at that store.

Part 6
Follow the lines and copy each word.

swim	locks
plant	plant
locks	swim

thing	lunch
sheets	thing
lunch	sheets

Part 7
Read the words and sentences.

to   do   desk   rest   rush   hub

what   when   then   town   swimming

sunny   sleeps   grabs   yes   you

1. His dad said, "Go to the store now."

2. Six green bugs hid under the rug.

3. I can not smell this plant.

☐ ☐ ☐ ☐ ☐ ☐

(Parent's/Listener's) signature _____ Date _____

Directions, Part 7:
1. Tell the student to read each row of words and the sentences.
2. Make a check mark in the box if the student reads all the words in the row or in the sentence correctly.

96   *Lesson 58*

Lesson 59

Name _____

Part 1
Draw the lines. Then write in the missing letters.

trips — chops
sold — black
north — sold
black — north
chops — trips

Part 2
Follow the lines and copy each sound.

n — s
r — n
s — i
a — r
c — a
i — c

Part 3
Draw lines to match the words and pictures.

stamp
stump
lamp

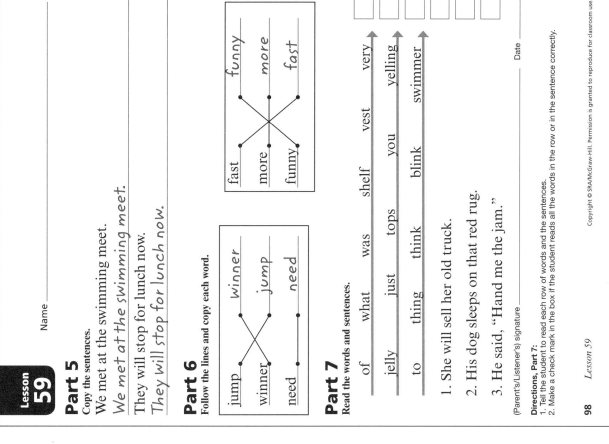

Part 4
Follow the lines and copy each word.

sleeps — letter
born — sleeps
told — born
shops — when
letter — told
when — shops

Part 5
Copy the sentences.

We met at the swimming meet.
We met at the swimming meet.

They will stop for lunch now.
They will stop for lunch now.

Part 6
Follow the lines and copy each word.

jump — winner
winner — jump
need — need

fast — funny
more — more
funny — fast

Part 7
Read the words and sentences.

of   what   was   shelf   vest   very

jelly   just   tops   you   yelling

to   thing   think   blink   swimmer

1. She will sell her old truck.

2. His dog sleeps on that red rug.

3. He said, "Hand me the jam."

(Parent's/Listener's) signature _____ Date _____

Directions, Part 7:
1. Tell the student to read each row of words and the sentences.
2. Make a check mark in the box if the student reads all the words in the row or in the sentence correctly.

98   Lesson 59

Copyright © SRA/McGraw-Hill. Permission is granted to reproduce for classroom use.

161

162

Lesson 60

Name _____

Part 1
Follow the lines and copy each sound.

h	th
th	a
wh	i
o	wh
i	h
a	o

Part 2
Draw the lines. Then write in the missing letters.

corn	clamp
jumps	trucks
clamp	think
trucks	corn
think	jumps

Part 3
Circle the sentence that tells about the picture.

He has pants that fit.

He has socks that fit.

He has pants that do not fit.

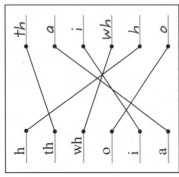

Part 4
Circle the words.

pin p a n l i p pin s h i p p e n i p p i t pin p i g p a n p e t pin
t r i p f i t p a n pin l i p p e n s pin p a t p e t pin p i g c l i p ⑥

Sound/symbol relationships, word completion, sentence reading, word matching

Lesson 60   **99**

Lesson 60

Name _____

Part 5
Follow the lines and copy each word.

trees	cold
north	trees
cold	north

sell	sell
grabs	stop
stop	grabs

Part 6
Copy the sentences.

He told me how to get to the store.
He told me how to get to the store.

Her dog sleeps on that old rug.
Her dog sleeps on that old rug.

Part 7
Read the words and sentences.

check	think	things	told	planting
morning	grips	lunch	stuck	steep
felt	very	jumping	was	wishing

□ □ □ □ □ □

1. She said, "When do you go to class?"

2. They sat down on an ant hill.

3. We will send a gift to her.

(Parent's/Listener's) signature _____ Date _____

Directions, Part 7:
1. Tell the student to read each row of words and the sentences.
2. Make a check mark in the box if the student reads all the words in the row or in the sentence correctly.

100   *Lesson 60*

Lesson 61

Name _____

Part 1
Draw the lines. Then write in the missing letters.

chops	fork
fork	under
jelly	stand
under	chops
stand	jelly

Part 2
Follow the lines and copy each sound.

er	c
or	y
c	or
w	er
y	n
n	w

Part 3
Circle the sentence that tells about the picture.

The frog sat next to the old truck.

(The frog sat on top of the old truck.)

The frog sat under the old truck.

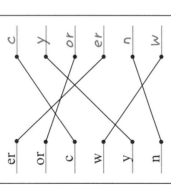

Part 4
Circle the words.

(belt) b e t b e l l b e l t w e l l f e l t (belt) b e l t l e n d f e l t (belt) l

b e t s f e l t t e l l (belt) f e l t s e l l l e f t s e n d (belt) l e f t e n d f e

Word completion, sound/symbol relationships, sentence reading, word matching

---

Lesson 61

Name _____

Part 5
Follow the lines and copy each word.

seeds	store
store	check
check	seeds

plant	told
things	plant
told	things

Part 6
Copy the sentences.

They had lots of desks in the class.

They had lots of desks in the class.

The horse ran on a dusty path.

The horse ran on a dusty path.

Part 7
Read the words and sentences.

butter	under	damp	after	mast
than	hold	when	clocks	you
stops	shop	what	lots	list

□ □ □ □ □ □

1. She was the best singer in town.

2. They sat on a hill next to the pond.

3. He said, "I feel much better now."

(Parent's/Listener's) signature _____ Date _____

Directions, Part 7:
1. Tell the student to read each row of words and the sentences.
2. Make a check mark in the box if the student reads all words in the row or in the sentence correctly.

163

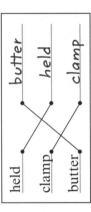

Lesson 62

Name _____

Part 1
Follow the lines and copy each sound.

u	a
a	ol
i	v
z	i
v	u
ol	z

Part 2
Draw the lines. Then write in the missing letters.

smell	check
after	smell
hold	town
check	after
town	hold

Part 3
Circle the sentence that tells about the picture.

(This clock will not run.)

This clock will run very well.

This clock did not stop.

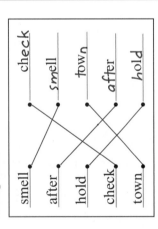

Part 4
Circle the words.

(wish) dish (wish) cash mi fish list (wish) will win (wish) w
in will fish (wish) mash mist last will (wish) with ⑤

Lesson 62

Name _____

Part 5
Follow the lines and copy each word.

held	butter
clamp	held
butter	clamp

block	much
much	sheep
sheep	block

Part 6
Copy the sentences.

You left lots of things on her desk.

You left lots of things on her desk.

Six men will camp on that hill.

Six men will camp on that hill.

Part 7
Read the words and sentences.

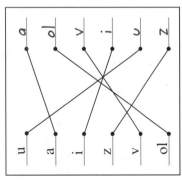

things	winner	chopping	what	after
slip	stuck	silly	clapping	spring
store	cold	lucky	very	shelf

1. Can we swim in that pond?

2. Bud said, "I will fix a big dinner."

3. Her left leg is in a cast.

_____ (Parent's/Listener's) signature   Date _____

104   *Lesson 62*

Lesson 63

Part 1
Draw the lines. Then write in the missing letters.

hands — *crash*
dust — *sheets*
sheets — *drop*
drop — *dust*
crash — *hands*

Part 2
Follow the lines and copy each word.

er — *n*
or — *er*
n — *v*
r — *or*
w — *r*
v — *w*

Part 3
Draw lines to match the words and pictures.

mast
cast
fist

Part 4
Follow the lines and copy each word.

best — *winner*
fans — *best*
crush — *fans*
things — *chops*
winner — *crush*
chops — *things*

Word completion, sound/symbol relationships, word recognition, copying words

---

Lesson 63

Part 5
Copy the sentences.

An old truck went down the street.
An old truck went down the street.
His black cat sat in his lap.
His black cat sat in his lap.

Part 6
Follow the lines and copy each word.

cold — *down*
shelf — *shelf*
down — *cold*

Part 7
Read the words and sentences.

think	spring	of	slick	you
planting	things	next	letters	do
stops	stamp	which	hammer	grip

1. Help her fix that clock now.
2. His mom said, "What did you do this morning?"
3. When did they get on the bus?

(Parent's/Listener's signature) _____ Date _____

Directions, Part 7:
1. Tell the student to read each row of words and the sentences.
2. Make a check mark in the box if the student reads all the words in the row or in the sentence correctly.

Page 166

Lesson 64

Name _____

Part 1
Follow the lines and copy each sound.

z	v
v	b
j	y
ch	j
y	z
b	ch

Part 2
Draw the lines. Then write in the missing letters.

fold	drink
which	fold
drink	which
stuck	more
more	stuck

Part 3
Draw lines to match the words and pictures.

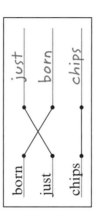

flag
frog
fork

Page 108

Lesson 64

Name _____

Part 5
Copy the sentences.

The wet street is slick.
The wet street is slick.

Her mom lost her green hat.
Her mom lost her green hat.

Part 6
Follow the lines and copy each word.

born	just
just	born
chips	chips

Part 4
Follow the lines and copy each word.

plants	much
shop	yell
think	shop
much	hold
yell	think
hold	plants

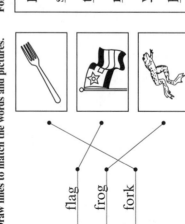

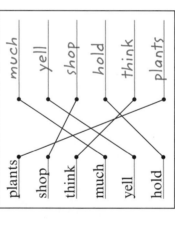

path	path
better	crash
crash	better

Part 7
Read the words and sentences.

□ □ □ □ □ □

funny	needs	lost	stops	store
stamps	stink	quick	which	shelf
rent	swinging	what	of	happy

1. Do not step on that rug with muddy feet.
2. When will we get to the next town?
3. She said, "I did not see you in math class."

(Parent's/Listener's) signature _____ Date _____

Directions, Part 7:
1. Tell the student to read each row of words and the sentences.
2. Make a check mark in the box if the student reads all the words in the row or in the sentence correctly.

108   *Lesson 64*

Copyright © SRA/McGraw-Hill. Permission is granted to reproduce for classroom use.

Lesson 65

Name _____

Part 1
Draw the lines. Then write in the missing letters.

sleeps	north
things	letter
north	hold
letter	sleeps
hold	things

Part 2
Follow the lines and copy each sound.

er	or
w	er
or	f
wh	w
ol	wh
f	ol

Part 3
Draw lines to match the words and pictures.

ring
fin
tent

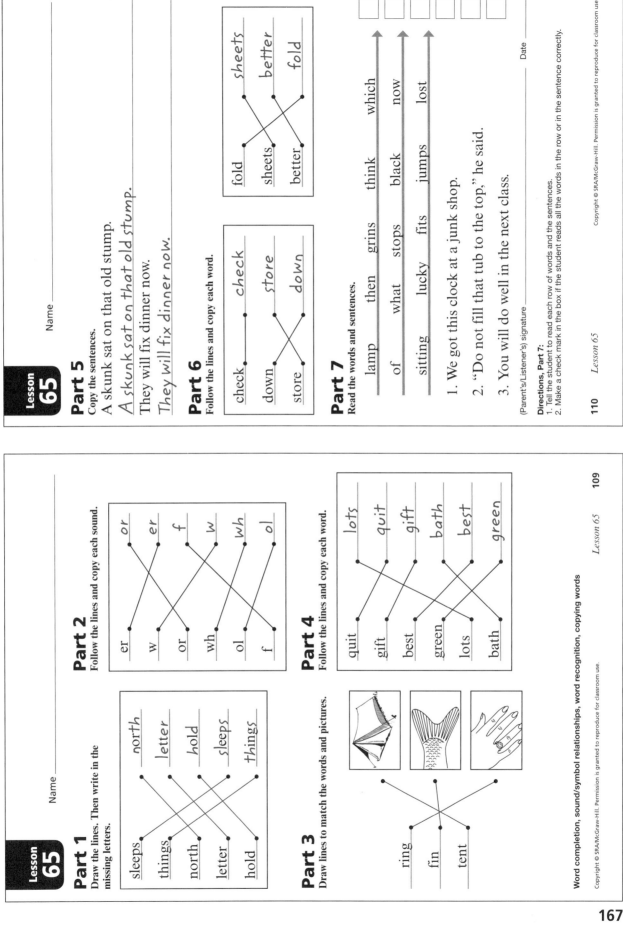

Part 4
Follow the lines and copy each word.

quit	lots
gift	quit
best	gift
green	bath
lots	best
bath	green

Word completion, sound/symbol relationships, word recognition, copying words

---

Lesson 65

Name _____

Part 5
Copy the sentences.

A skunk sat on that old stump.

A skunk sat on that old stump.

They will fix dinner now.

They will fix dinner now.

Part 6
Follow the lines and copy each word.

check	check
down	store
store	down

fold	sheets
sheets	better
better	fold

Part 7
Read the words and sentences.

lamp	then	grins	think	which
of	what	stops	black	now
sitting	lucky	fits	jumps	lost

☐ ☐ ☐ ☐ ☐ ☐

1. We got this clock at a junk shop.

2. "Do not fill that tub to the top," he said.

3. You will do well in the next class.

_____ Date _____
(Parent's/Listener's) signature

Directions, Part 7:
1. Tell the student to read each row of words and the sentences.
2. Make a check mark in the box if the student reads all the words in the row or in the sentence correctly.